D1102763

Heinemann PSYCHOLOGY AS *for OCR*

Heinemann
PSYCHOLOGY AS
for OCR

Fiona Lintern Lynne Williams Alan Hill

Heinemann

Inspiring generations

Heinemann Educational Publishers
Halley Court, Jordan Hill, Oxford OX2 8EJ
Part of Harcourt Education

Heinemann is the registered trademark of
Harcourt Education Limited

© Fiona Lintern, Lynne Williams and Alan Hill, 2003

First published 2003

07 06 05 04
10 9 8 7 6 5 4 3 2 1

British Library Cataloguing in Publication Data is available
from the British Library on request.

ISBN 0435 807064

Series Editor: David Moxon

Edited by Susan Ross

Typeset and illustrated by 🔺 Tek-Art, Croydon

Original illustrations © Harcourt Education Limited, 2002

Cover illustration by Matt Buckley

Printed in the UK by Bath Press Ltd

Picture research by Thelma Gilbert

Acknowledgements
The authors would like to dedicate this book to Sam, Jamie, Caitlin, Megan and Elli, with all
our love.

The publishers would like to thank the British Psychological Society for permission to
reproduce copyright material on the CD-ROM.

Every effort has been made to contact copyright holders of material reproduced in this book.
Any omissions will be rectified in subsequent printings if notice is given to the publishers.

The publishers would like to thank the following for permission to reproduce photographs:
Corbis: pp. 18, 34, 106; Ronald Grant: p. 29; Hulton Archive: pp. 62, 105; Magnum
Photos/Paul Fusco: p. 36; Alexandra Milgram: pp. 100, 101, 102; Oxford Scientific Films: p.39;
SPL: pp. 50, 88; Popperfoto: pp. 51, 135; Rex Features: p. 113; RGA: p. 147; Science Photo
Library: pp. 56, 76, 80, 91, 94; Topham Picturepoint: pp. 57, 86; Philip Zimbardo: p. 110.

Websites
There are links to relevant websites in this book. In order to ensure that the links are up
to date, that they work, and that the sites are not inadvertently linked to sites that could
be considered offensive, we have made the links available on the Heinemann website at
www.heinemann.co.uk/hotlinks. When you access the site, the express code is: 670XP.

Tel: 01865 888058 www.heinemann.co.uk

Contents

Book

Chapter 1	Introduction	
What is psychology?		
The core studies		
The OCR AS Psychology examinations		
Thinking like a psychologist (1): methods		
Thinking like a psychologist (2): themes		
Thinking like a psychologist (3): ethics		
Useful resources		

Chapter 2	The cognitive approach	
The core studies		
Section 1	Loftus and Palmer (1974): background	
Section 2	Loftus and Palmer (1974): the core study	
Section 3	Thinking like a psychologist – evaluating the core study	
Section 4	Deregowski (1972): background	
Section 5	Deregowski (1972): the core study	
Section 6	Thinking like a psychologist – evaluating the core study	
Section 7	Baron-Cohen, Leslie and Frith (1985): background	
Section 8	Baron-Cohen, Leslie and Frith (1985): the core study	
Section 9	Thinking like a psychologist – evaluating the core study	
Section 10	Gardner and Gardner (1969): background	
Section 11	Gardner and Gardner (1969): the core study	
Section 12	Thinking like a psychologist – evaluating the core study	
Useful resources		

Chapter 3	The developmental approach	
The core studies		
Section 1	Samuel and Bryant (1984): background	
Section 2	Samuel and Bryant (1984): the core study	
Section 3	Thinking like a psychologist – evaluating the core study	

CD

	Introduction	1
1	Key people in the development of psychology	
2	Career opportunities for psychologists	
4	Useful web addresses	
6	The British Psychological Society's Code of Conduct	
8	Who's Who	
10		
12		

	The cognitive approach	13
15	Clive Wearing	
16	Free recall versus recognition	
18	Eye-witness testimony experiment	
20	Photofit faces	
22	Gardner and Gardner – Project Washoe	
24	Deregowski	
26		
28		
30		
32		
34		
36		
38		
40		

	The developmental approach	41
43	Harlow's research	
44	Attachment in a children's home	
46	Freud's psychosexual stages	
48	Freudian dreams	

Contents

Section 4	Bandura, Ross and Ross (1961): background	50	Classical conditioning
Section 5	Bandura, Ross and Ross (1961): the core study	52	Operant conditioning: technical terms
Section 6	Thinking like a psychologist – evaluating the core study	54	Freud
Section 7	Hodges and Tizard (1989): background	56	Bandura's experiment
Section 8	Hodges and Tizard (1989): the core study	58	
Section 9	Thinking like a psychologist – evaluating the core study	60	
Section 10	Freud (1909): background	62	
Section 11	Freud (1909): the core study	64	
Section 12	Thinking like a psychologist – evaluating the core study	66	
Useful resources		68	

Chapter 4	The physiological approach	69	The physiological approach
The core studies		71	The human nervous system
Section 1	Schachter and Singer (1962): background	72	Personality and stress
Section 2	Schachter and Singer (1962): the core study	74	Stress and the workplace
Section 3	Thinking like a psychologist – evaluating the core study	76	Sperry
			Raine
Section 4	Dement and Kleitman (1957): background	78	Dement and Kleitman
Section 5	Dement and Kleitman (1957): the core study	80	PET scans
Section 6	Thinking like a psychologist – evaluating the core study	82	EEG and the measurement of brain activity
Section 7	Sperry (1968): background	84	
Section 8	Sperry (1968): the core study	86	
Section 9	Thinking like a psychologist – evaluating the core study	88	
Section 10	Raine, Buchsbaum and LaCasse (1997): background	90	
Section 11	Raine, Buchsbaum and LaCasse (1997): the core study	92	
Section 12	Thinking like a psychologist – evaluating the core study	94	
Useful resources		96	

Contents

Chapter 5	The social approach	97	The social approach
The core studies		99	The Stanford prison simulation
Section 1	Milgram (1963): background	100	Haney, Banks and Zimbardo
Section 2	Milgram (1963): the core study	102	Milgram's experiment
Section 3	Thinking like a psychologist – evaluating the core study	104	Milgram
			Conformity in daily life
Section 4	Haney, Banks and Zimbardo (1973): background	106	General issues in Milgram
			Obedience in real life
Section 5	Haney, Banks and Zimbardo (1973): the core study	108	Piliavin
			Tajfel
Section 6	Thinking like a psychologist – evaluating the core study	110	Blue Eyes Brown Eyes
Section 7	Piliavin, Rodin and Piliavin (1969): background	112	
Section 8	Piliavin, Rodin and Piliavin (1969): the core study	114	
Section 9	Thinking like a psychologist – evaluating the core study	116	
Section 10	Tajfel (1970): background	118	
Section 11	Tajfel (1970): the core study	120	
Section 12	Thinking like a psychologist – evaluating the core study	122	
Useful resources		124	
Chapter 6	The individual differences approach	125	The individual differences approach
The core studies		127	
Section 1	Gould (1982): background	128	Historical treatments for mental illness
Section 2	Gould (1982): the core study	130	Culture-bound syndromes
Section 3	Thinking like a psychologist – evaluating the core study	132	Gould
Section 4	Hraba and Grant (1970): background	134	The Three Faces of Eve
Section 5	Hraba and Grant (1970): the core study	136	Rosenhan
Section 6	Thinking like a psychologist – evaluating the core study	138	
Section 7	Rosenhan (1973): background	140	
Section 8	Rosenhan (1973): the core study	142	
Section 9	Thinking like a psychologist – evaluating the core study	144	

Contents

Section 10   Thigpen and Cleckley (1954): background   146
Section 11   Thigpen and Cleckley (1954): the core study   148
Section 12   Thinking like a psychologist – evaluating the   150
             core study
Useful resources   152

Chapter 7   Psychological investigations   **153**

Activity A   Questions, self-reports and questionnaires   156
             Preparing for the exam: evaluating Activity A   158
Activity B   An observation   160
             Preparing for the exam: evaluating Activity B   162
Activity C   Comparison of data to investigate the difference   164
             between two conditions
             Preparing for the exam: evaluating Activity C   166
Activity D   Correlation   168
             Preparing for the exam: evaluating Activity D   170
An introduction to statistics   172
Key concepts   174
Useful resources   175

Psychological investigations

Data Analysis 1
Data Analysis 2
Data Analysis 3
Aims and hypotheses
Hypotheses and significance

Revision

Crosswords
Cognitive approach
Developmental approach
Physiological approach
Social approach
Individual differences approach

Exam questions

Questions – Core Studies 1
   (2540)
Questions – Core Studies 2
   (2541)
Questions – Psychological
   Investigations (2542)
Mark Scheme – Core Studies 1
   (2540)
Mark Scheme – Core Studies 2
   (2541)
Mark Scheme – Psychological
   Investigations (2542)

CHAPTER I

INTRODUCTION

WHAT IS PSYCHOLOGY?

Psychology is the study of human behaviour and experience. Psychologists study a range of fascinating topics, which include:

- Cognitive processes, such as memory and language;
- Developmental issues such as the development of intelligence, how children learn and what is necessary for 'normal' development;
- Social issues such as obedience, conformity to social roles, helping behaviour and prejudice;
- Physiological processes such as sleep and dreaming, emotion and the relationship between brain activity and behaviour; and
- Individual differences, such as intelligence testing, racial self-identification, abnormality, and mental health issues.

All of these topics and more are included in the OCR AS Psychology course.

How do I study Psychology?

If you are going to succeed at AS Psychology, you will need to develop critical thinking skills. This means reading the material carefully and thinking about the issues that are raised. For example, you may be able to spot flaws in the way the researchers conducted their research, or you may be able to think about practical applications that arise from the research.

We have tried to make this as easy as possible for you, by highlighting all the relevant issues as we discuss the studies. We hope that you enjoy studying psychology and that you find this book and CD-ROM useful.

CD-ROM

Introduction: Key people in the development of psychology

THE CORE STUDIES

The OCR AS Psychology specification looks at 20 original pieces of research. This book gives you the background to each piece of research, a summary of the core study, followed by a detailed evaluation. Exam hints are given throughout and suggestions for further reading and Internet resources are given at the end of each section.

THE CORE STUDIES

The 20 core studies are listed below.

The Cognitive Approach

Loftus, E. F. and Palmer, J. C. (1974) 'Reconstruction of automobile destruction: An example of the interaction between language and memory', *Journal of Verbal Learning and Verbal Behaviour*, 13, 585–9.

Deregowski, J. B. (1972) 'Pictorial perception and culture', *Scientific American*, 227, 82–8.

Baron-Cohen, S., Leslie, A.M. and Frith, U. (1985) 'Does the autistic child have a "theory of mind"?', *Cognition*, 21, 37–46.

Gardner, R. A. and Gardner, B. T. (1969) 'Teaching sign language to a chimpanzee', *Science*, 165, 664–72.

The Developmental Approach

Samuel, J. and Bryant, P. (1984) 'Asking only one question in the conservation experiment', *Journal of Child Psychology and Psychiatry*, 25, 315–18.

Bandura, A., Ross, D. and Ross, S. A. (1961) 'Transmission of aggression through imitation of aggressive models', *Journal of Abnormal and Social Psychology*, 63, 575–82.

Hodges, J. and Tizard, B. (1989b) 'Social and family relationships of ex-institutional adolescents', *Journal of Child Psychology and Psychiatry*, 30, 77–97.

Freud, S. (1909) 'Analysis of a phobia of a five-year-old boy' in *The Pelican Freud Library* (1977), vol. 8, Case Histories 1, pp. 169–306.

The Physiological Approach

Schachter, S. and Singer, J. E. (1962) 'Cognitive, social and physiological determinants of emotional state', *Psychological Review*, 69, 379–99.

Dement, W. and Kleitman, N. (1957) 'The relation of eye movements during sleep to dream activity: An objective method for the study of dreaming', *Journal of Experimental Psychology*, 53, 339–46.

Sperry, R. W. (1968) 'Hemisphere deconnection and unity in consciousness', *American Psychologist*, 23, 723–33.

Raine, A., Buchsbaum, M. and LaCasse, L. (1997) 'Brain abnormalities in murderers indicated by positron emission tomography', *Biological Psychiatry*, 42 (6), 495–508.

The Social Approach

Milgram, S. (1963) 'Behavioural study of obedience', *Journal of Abnormal and Social Psychology*, 67, 371–8.

Haney, C., Banks, W. C. and Zimbardo, P.G. (1973) 'A study of prisoners and guards in a simulated prison', *Naval Research Review*, 30, 4–17.

Piliavin, I. M., Rodin, J. A. and Piliavin, J. (1969) 'Good Samaritanism: An underground phenomenon?', *Journal of Personality and Social Psychology*, 13, 289–99.

Tajfel, H. (1970) 'Experiments in intergroup discrimination', *Scientific American*, 223, 96–102.

The Psychology of Individual Differences

Gould, S. J. (1982) 'A nation of morons', *New Scientist*, 6 May 1982, 349–52.

Hraba, J. and Grant, G. (1970) 'Black is beautiful: A re-examination of racial preference and identification', *Journal of Personality and Social Psychology*, 16, 398–402.

Rosenhan, D. L. (1973) 'On being sane in insane places', *Science*, 179, 250–58.

Thigpen, C. H. and Cleckley, H. (1954) 'A case of multiple personality', *Journal of Abnormal and Social Psychology*, 49, 135–51.

THE OCR AS PSYCHOLOGY EXAMINATIONS

You will sit three unit tests, each of one hour. These may be spread out throughout the year or you may sit them all together.

CORE STUDIES 1 (1 HOUR)

This consists of 20 short questions worth either 2 or 4 marks. There will be one question on each core study. The questions test your knowledge and understanding of the studies. This means that you could be asked about anything that appears in the studies or about issues relating to the concepts or methods used in the studies.

You could be asked about:
* the information in the studies
* the methods used in the studies
* the way the results are analysed and presented
* the conclusions that can be drawn from the studies
* the context of the studies
* the general psychological issues illustrated by the studies
* evaluations of all the above.

There is some discussion of methodological issues later in this introduction. Methodology is also discussed in Chapter 7 and each core study is followed by a discussion which includes comments on methods.

CORE STUDIES 2 (1 HOUR)

This paper has two sections. In the first section, you answer one question from a choice of two. These are longer questions and each question gives you a choice of one of three core studies to write about. In the second section, you answer one question from a choice of two and you have to write about four of the core studies which are named.

The questions in this paper concentrate on themes and perspectives.

Themes
* Application of psychology to everyday life
* Determinism
* Ecological validity
* Ethics
* Ethnocentric bias
* Individual and situational explanations
* Nature and nurture
* Psychometrics
* Qualitative and quantitative measures

- Reductionism
- Reinforcement
- Reliability and validity
- Social control
- Usefulness of psychological research

Each of these themes is explained on pages 8–9.

Perspectives

Approaches in psychology:
- cognitive (Chapter 2)
- developmental (Chapter 3)
- physiological (Chapter 4)
- social (Chapter 5)
- individual differences (Chapter 6).

These perspectives are discussed throughout each chapter.

PSYCHOLOGICAL INVESTIGATIONS (1 HOUR)

During the AS course, you will carry our four data collecting activities, which are as follows:
- Activity A: Questions, self-reports and questionnaires.
- Activity B: An observation.
- Activity C: Collection of data to investigate the difference between two conditions.
- Activity D: Collection of data involving two independent measures and analysis using a test of correlation.

You record notes on these activities in a **Practical Investigations Folder** which will be given to you. You may take this into the examination and refer to it. The exam will ask you for some of the information in the folder (for example the aim, results and conclusions of your activity) but will also ask you questions about strengths and weaknesses of your activity and possible improvements, and their effects. Further details on this unit are given in Chapter 7.

THINKING LIKE A PSYCHOLOGIST (1): METHODS

Psychologists use a variety of research methods when conducting their research. The core studies include experiments, observations, case studies, self-report measures, psychometric tests and review articles.

EXPERIMENTAL METHODS

All experimental methods involve the manipulation of an **independent variable (IV)** to see its effect on the **dependent variable (DV)**.

Laboratory experiments

In a laboratory experiment the experimenter deliberately manipulates the IV and maintains strict control over all other variables. The core study by Loftus and Palmer is an example of a laboratory experiment.

Field experiments

Field experiments are carried out in a natural environment, but the IV is still manipulated by the experimenter. The core study by Piliavin *et al.* is a field experiment.

Natural experiments

Natural experiments (or **quasi-experiments**) take place in circumstances which allow the researcher to examine the effect of a naturally occurring IV (often used where artificial manipulation would be impossible or unethical). The core study by Hodges and Tizard and the study by Sperry are examples of natural experiments.

OBSERVATIONAL METHODS

Psychologists often simply observe behaviour in real-life situations or in the laboratory without manipulating an IV. Observations involve the precise measurement of behaviour in an objective way.

Some studies are entirely observational but, more frequently, researchers use observation as a way of recording behaviour as part of an experiment (the core study by Bandura and the study by Rosenhan are good examples of research that uses observational methods).

QUESTIONING PEOPLE

There are several different ways in which people can be questioned. They may be interviewed face to face or complete a questionnaire themselves. Questions may be **closed** (yes/no) or **open**. Open questions are more flexible and do not try to put people into pre-prepared

KEY DEFINITIONS

The strengths of laboratory experiments are:
- high levels of control over extraneous variables
- cause and effect relationships can be established
- they are easy to replicate (repeat).

The weaknesses of laboratory experiments are:
- low ecological validity
- participants may be subject to demand characteristics
- samples may not be representative.

The strengths of field experiments are:
- greater ecological validity
- lower demand characteristics (if people are not aware they are being studied).

The weaknesses are:
- they are harder to control
- they are difficult to replicate
- they may be unethical (if people are not aware they are being studied).

The strengths of natural experiments are:
- greater ecological validity (real groups)
- they allow researchers to investigate areas that would otherwise be unavailable to them.

The weaknesses are:
- it is difficult to infer cause and effect (since no control)
- they are impossible to replicate exactly.

The strengths of observational methods are:
- high ecological validity (in real life)
- they can be used when experimental research would be impossible.

The weaknesses are:
- cause and effect cannot be established
- they are very difficult to replicate.

The strengths of closed questions are:
- they are easy to quantify and analyse
- they are reliable, easy to replicate and generalisable.

The weaknesses are:
- data may be distorted due to restricted answers
- demand characteristics may be high
- some important information may be missed.

The strengths of case studies are:
- they produce highly detailed data
- they are particularly appropriate for the study of 'exceptional' cases
- they are often used in therapeutic contexts.

The weaknesses are:
- they cannot be generalised to the wider population
- they cannot be replicated
- the researcher may be biased.

The strengths of review articles are:
- large amounts of data can be examined
- they bring research together, often for the first time
- they are easier to access than many original papers.

The weaknesses are:
- studies being reviewed may be flawed
- the reviewer may be biased
- it is difficult to ensure that a representative sample of all the relevant literature is reviewed.

categories, but they are more much time consuming and difficult to analyse.

People may also be questioned using **psychometric tests** such as personality and IQ tests which, when standardised, are easy to administer and score, and allow researchers to make comparisons between individuals. However, it is difficult to construct reliable and valid tests.

CASE STUDIES

Case studies are in-depth studies of individuals (and sometimes groups). They are often used to study unusual examples of behaviour and may provide important insights into psychological theories. The core studies by Freud (Little Hans) and Thigpen and Cleckley (Three Faces of Eve) are examples of case studies.

REVIEW ARTICLES

Such articles are produced when researchers do not obtain their own data (primary data) but instead read and review studies already published and then draw general conclusions from these. The core studies by Deregowski and by Gould are examples of review articles.

THINKING LIKE A PSYCHOLOGIST (2): THEMES

Each of the themes below should be considered in relation to as many of the core studies as possible. In the section 'Thinking like a psychologist' which follows each of the core studies, several themes are discussed.

THE THEMES

Application of psychology to everyday life

To what extent can we explain everyday behaviours using the results of the core studies?

Determinism

This is the argument that our behaviour is determined (decided) by factors outside of our control. Behaviour may be determined by biological factors such as genes or hormones, or by situational factors such as reinforcements (see page 9) that we receive from others. The opposite argument is the free-will argument which states that individuals are free to choose how to behave.

Ecological validity

If a piece of research is high in ecological validity, it is easy to relate to real life. For example, an experiment conducted in realistic conditions would be said to be high in ecological validity and an experiment conducted in artificial conditions would be said to be low in ecological validity.

Ethics

The British Psychological Society (BPS) issues Ethical Guidelines for those involved in psychological research. The guidelines are a set of rules outlining what is acceptable and what is not acceptable in research. For example, participants in psychological research should give their informed consent before the research starts, should not be deceived or distressed in any way and should have their right to withdraw from the research made clear to them.

Ethnocentric bias

This is the tendency to interpret human behaviour from the viewpoint of our own ethnic, social or other group. This can lead to serious problems of 'scientific racism'. The term ethnocentrism is used to refer to the tendency to favour our own group over others.

Individual and situational explanations

This refers to the way we explain behaviour. An individual explanation would be 'something about the person' (he fell over because he was

FOR CONSIDERATION

Why do you think that it is important that a piece of research has high ecological validity?

CD-ROM

Introduction: The British Psychological Society's Code of Conduct

clumsy) and a situational explanation would be 'something about the situation' (she fell over because the floor was slippery). Some psychologists favour individual explanations of behaviour and some prefer situational explanations.

Do you think that human behaviour is a result of nature or nurture, or a combination of the two?

Nature and nurture

This is a very important debate in psychology and concerns the relative influences of inheritance and experience. Nature refers to the inherited or genetic make-up of a person and nurture refers to all other influences from the moment of conception.

Psychometrics

Psychometric tests measure 'mental' characteristics. These include intelligence and personality and also aptitudes for certain jobs and tendencies towards anti-social behaviours.

Qualitative and quantitative measures

Quantitative measures are numeric. Much research records behaviour in quantitative ways, for example by counting the number of aggressive acts, or by asking people to rate their own behaviours or feelings on numerical scales. Qualitative measures do not use numbers and rely more on descriptions and interpretations of behaviour. Some research simply describes the behaviour of individuals and an alternative to a numerical rating scale would be a more open-ended question where people simply describe how they feel.

Reductionism

This involves explaining complex psychological phenomena by reducing them to a much simpler level, often focusing on a single factor.

Reinforcement

A reinforcer is something that increases the likelihood of a behaviour occurring again. This may be in the form of a pleasant consequence such as praise or may be the avoidance of unpleasant experiences.

Reliability

This may be described as consistency. If a measure is reliable, it will give you consistent results.

Validity

Does a measure actually measure what it claims to be measuring?

Social control

This involves attempts to influence the behaviour of people and is the extent to which a piece of research contributes to human welfare.

THINKING LIKE A PSYCHOLOGIST (3): ETHICS

The British Psychological Society (BPS) issues Ethical Guidelines for those involved in conducting psychological research. You should consider the ethics of each of the core studies in relation to the summary below and decide whether the research conducted was ethical or not.

GENERAL

Investigators must consider the **ethical implications** and **psychological consequences** for the participants in their research. Threats to their psychological well-being, health, values or dignity should be eliminated.

CONSENT

Whenever possible, the investigator should *inform* all participants of the objectives of the investigation.

Research with children or with participants who have impairments that will limit understanding and/or communication such that they are unable to give their own consent requires special safeguarding procedures.

When research involves anyone under 16 years of age, consent should be obtained from parents or carers.

Investigators should realise that they are often in a position of authority or influence over participants who may be their students, employees or clients. This relationship must not be allowed to pressurise the participants to take part in, or remain in, an investigation.

The payment of participants must not be used to persuade them to take risks beyond the ones they would have been prepared to take without payment.

DECEPTION

The withholding of information or the misleading of participants is unacceptable if the participants are likely to object or to show unease once debriefed.

Participants should never be deliberately misled without extremely strong scientific or medical justification.

DEBRIEFING

Debriefing does not provide a justification for unethical aspects of any investigation. Some effects which may be produced by an experiment

HOT EXAM HINTS

You will also have to work within these guidelines when you conduct your own activities. For more details, see Chapter 7.

CD-ROM

Introduction: The British Psychological Society's Code of Conduct

FOR CONSIDERATION

The core studies by Milgram, Bandura, Piliavin et al and Rosenhan all raise issues of informed consent. Do you think that researchers should be able to study people without their consent?

The core studies by Schachter and Singer and Milgram involved deception. Why might researchers deceive their participants?

will not be cancelled out by this process. Investigators have to ensure that participants receive any necessary debriefing in the form of active intervention before they leave the research setting.

WITHDRAWAL FROM THE INVESTIGATION

At the start of the investigation, investigators should make plain to participants their right to withdraw from the research at any time, irrespective of whether or not payment or any other inducement has been offered.

CONFIDENTIALITY

Information obtained about a participant during an investigation is confidential unless otherwise agreed in advance.

PROTECTION OF PARTICIPANTS

Investigators have a responsibility to protect participants from physical and mental harm. Where research may involve behaviour or experiences that participants may regard as personal and private, the participants must be protected from stress, and should be assured that answers to personal questions need not be given.

In research involving children, investigators should act with caution when discussing the results with parents, teachers, etc.

OBSERVATIONAL RESEARCH

Unless those observed give their consent to being observed, observational research is only acceptable in situations where those observed could expect to be observed by strangers.

FOR CONSIDERATION

In Milgram's study, would it have made any difference to the results if participants had been clearly told that they could leave at any time?

Did the following researchers do everything they could to protect their participants: Bandura et al., Haney, Banks and Zimbardo?

USEFUL RESOURCES

BOOKS

Other textbooks that cover the OCR AS specification include:

Gross, R. (2003) *Key Studies in Psychology*, Hodder & Stoughton, 4th edn.
This book includes virtually complete versions of all 20 core studies.
Ideal for extra reading although some of the studies are harder to read
than others. Has excellent evaluation sections.

Banyard, P. and Grayson, A. (2000) *Introducing Psychological Research*, Palgrave.
This book has short, easy-to-read summaries of the 20 core studies and
many more. There are also questions and suggested answers.

Oliver, K. (2000) *Psychology and Everyday Life*, Hodder & Stoughton.
This book also includes summaries of each of the 20 studies and plenty
of background information. It is very easy to read.

Lintern, F. (2003) *Student's Handbook for OCR Psychology AS Level*,
Hodder and Stoughton.
This is not a textbook but a study guide. There are very short
summaries of the studies included and lots of revision activities.

Hill, G. (2002) *AS Psychology through Diagrams*, Oxford Revision
Guides, Oxford University Press.
This is also a revision book. It includes one-page 'schematic' summaries
of each of the core studies and lots more useful information.

Philip Allan Updates also publishes *Student Unit Guides* for core
studies 1 and 2 and for psychological investigations which are written
by experienced examiners and include lots of useful exam hints.

Banyard, P. (1999) *Controversies in Psychology*, Routledge Modular
Psychology Series, Routledge.
An excellent introduction to some key themes and debates in psychology.

WEBSITES

Go to www.heinemann.co.uk/hotlinks and insert the code 670XP.
Look at the websites listed under Introduction: Useful websites.

CD-ROM

Introduction: Useful web addresses and career opportunities

TIPS FOR USING THE INTERNET

There are literally thousands of psychology websites so choose your search words carefully. You can find sites by searching for the names of the authors of the core studies as well as searching for topics. Sites that end in 'ac' are academic sites (such as universities) and will contain reliable information.

CHAPTER 2 THE COGNITIVE APPROACH

THE CORE STUDIES

WHAT IS COGNITIVE PSYCHOLOGY?

Cognitive psychology studies mental processes such as memory, perception, thinking, reasoning, problem solving and language. These processes are not readily available for study as we can only guess what is happening inside someone's head by observing their behaviour. We cannot see thinking or memory; we can only see the end results of these processes as they are displayed in behaviour. This means that psychologists have to use a variety of techniques to study cognitive processes. The core studies considered in this chapter give a flavour of the range of research that is conducted.

THE CORE STUDIES

Loftus and Palmer (1974)

This is a laboratory study which examines the effect of leading questions on memory. The researchers conclude that very small changes to the way that questions are asked can have significant effects on what is recalled.

Deregowski (1972)

This core study is a review of research conducted by other researchers. Deregowski brings together a number of pieces of anecdotal and experimental evidence to address the question of whether pictures are a universal language. His conclusions are that there are many differences in the way different cultures produce and perceive pictures and therefore it is not possible to regard pictures as a universal language.

Baron-Cohen, Leslie and Frith (1985)

This core study uses a quasi-experimental design to compare groups of autistic, Down's syndrome and developmentally normal children in a false belief task. The authors conclude that a lack of theory of mind (the ability to understand that other people have thoughts and beliefs and that these may be different) is one of the core cognitive problems associated with autism.

Gardner and Gardner (1969)

This is a case study of one of the earliest attempts to teach sign language to a chimpanzee. The authors claim that Washoe learned to use 30 signs in the first 22 months of the study and that she demonstrated some of the criteria for language use.

LOFTUS AND PALMER (1974): BACKGROUND

WHAT IS MEMORY?

Without the ability to store and recall information, life would be impossible. No learning would take place and we would experience everything as if for the first time. When something is learned, a physical change takes place in the brain, leaving a memory 'trace' called an **engram**.

HOW LONG DOES MEMORY LAST?

One of the best supported models of memory distinguishes between three memory stores. These are:

- **sensory memory** which stores information for fractions of a second when it is first registered by our senses
- **short-term memory** which stores the information we attend to from our senses for around 15–30 seconds
- **long-term memory** which stores material for minutes, hours, weeks, months and even for a whole lifetime.

The model in Fig. 2.1 has been criticised for being too simplistic and not taking into consideration the different ways in which different types of information are stored. The model does not explain how information is transferred from one store to the next or how information can travel backwards from long-term to short-term memory (information in our long-term memory is necessary for us to understand what we are dealing with in short-term memory). More importantly, for the core study you are about to consider, there are many reasons why our memory of something may not be accurate.

WHAT FACTORS AFFECT OUR MEMORY?

The following factors are just a few of those that have been identified by psychologists.

Expectations/stereotypes

In a classic study conducted by Allport and Postman (1947) participants were shown a picture of two men arguing. The picture showed a well-dressed black man and a more casually dressed white man holding a cut-throat razor. After a very brief look at the picture, participants had to describe the picture to someone who hadn't seen it and they, in turn, had to describe it to someone else. The description rapidly changed to one in which the black man held the razor. This shows the **power of assumptions and stereotypes** to affect what is stored in our memory.

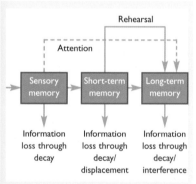

Fig. 2.1 Multi-store model of memory

Motivation

Freud suggested that we may be motivated to forget information which is disturbing or unpleasant. He called this repression.

Prevention of consolidation

Yarnell and Lynch (1973) found that American football players suffering from concussion were able to describe the events leading up to their injury if they were asked immediately afterwards. However, if they were not asked for 20 minutes, they had no memory of these events. This shows that it is necessary to have a period of time for biochemical/structural changes to occur in the brain which mean that the memory is stored. This is called **consolidation** and as well as being disrupted by head injury, this can also be affected by brain damage or surgery, electro-convulsive therapy and some drugs.

Interference

Later information can affect memories we already have. For example, if you were to get a new telephone number, it may not be long before you forget the old one.

Information received 'after the event'

Although the memory of an event is stored at the time of the event, research suggests that what has been stored can still change. The types of 'after the event' information that have been studied include the way witnesses are asked questions. Loftus and Zanni (1975) showed that people were more likely to recall seeing a broken headlight if the question was 'Did you see the broken headlight?' rather than 'Did you see a broken headlight?'. However, it is possible that this simply reflects participants giving the answers they think they should give rather than supporting the notion that their memory has actually changed. This has obvious implications for **eye-witness testimony**.

Why are psychologists interested in eye-witness testimony?

Juries are very convinced by eye-witness accounts and will tend to return guilty verdicts when there has been an eye-witness account presented by the prosecution. Even when the eye witness has been discredited in some way, juries still tend to be convinced by this information. Psychological research into memory strongly suggests that there are many factors which would make eye witnesses unreliable and the Devlin Committee (1973) recommended that juries should be instructed that it is not safe to convict on the basis of eye-witness testimony alone. The core study outlined in the next section is one of many research studies which demonstrate the unreliability of eye-witness memory.

Fig. 2.2 An eye-witness testimony

LOFTUS AND PALMER (1974): THE CORE STUDY

WHAT WAS THE AIM OF THE STUDY?

The aim of the study was to see if questions asked after an event can cause a reconstruction in one's memory of that event.

HOW WAS THE RESEARCH CARRIED OUT?

Loftus and Palmer used two laboratory experiments to investigate the effect of leading questions on recall.

Fig. 2.3 Elizabeth Loftus

CD-ROM

The Cognitive Approach: Eye-witness testimony.

Study 1

Forty-five student participants were shown seven clips of traffic accidents. After viewing each clip, the students were given a questionnaire which asked them to 'give an account of the accident you have just seen' and to answer specific questions. One of these questions is referred to as the **critical** question and it asked about the speed of the vehicles. The students were divided into five groups of nine participants and each group was asked a slightly different critical question:

Group 1: 'About how fast were the cars going when they **smashed** into each other?'

Group 2: 'About how fast were the cars going when they **collided** with each other?'

Group 3: 'About how fast were the cars going when they **bumped** each other?'

Group 4: 'About how fast were the cars going when they **hit** each other?'

Group 5: 'About how fast were the cars going when they **contacted** with each other?'

Average ratings of speeds for each condition were:
- smashed – 40.8 mph
- collided – 39.3 mph
- bumped – 38.1 mph
- hit – 34.0 mph
- contacted – 31.8 mph.

Fig. 2.4 How fast were the cars going?

Loftus and Palmer concluded from this that the wording of the question did affect the estimate of speed, with the more severe sounding verbs producing the higher estimates. When the question had the word 'smashed' in it, people gave estimates which were, on average, 9 mph higher than when the question was asked using the word 'contacted'.

How do Loftus and Palmer explain these results?

They suggest that there are two possible explanations for this finding.

The first possible explanation is **response bias factors**. This means that

FOR CONSIDERATION

- What other kinds of information might people 'remember'?
- The second study conducted by Loftus and Palmer investigates the second explanation. Is it possible to cause a distortion in someone's memory so that they will 'remember' something that wasn't there or didn't happen?

the participant consciously biases their response in the direction of the verb used in the question. In other words, they give the answer that they think the researchers want (**demand characteristics**).

The second possible explanation is that the question causes an actual distortion in the participant's memory of the event. The word 'smashed' leads the participant to recall the accident as being more severe than it actually was. From this explanation they propose that participants might also be more likely to 'remember' other details that did not actually occur but 'fit' with the 'memory' of the accident having occurred at high speed.

Study 2

This study was very similar to the first study: 150 student participants saw a one-minute film which contained a four-second scene of a multiple car accident and were then questioned about it. In this study, there were three groups. The independent variable (IV) is still the verb used in the question but the dependent variable (DV) is whether or not participants recall seeing broken glass:

- 50 subjects were asked 'How fast were the cars going when they *hit* each other?'.
- 50 subjects were asked 'How fast were the cars going when they *smashed* into each other?'.
- 50 subjects were not asked about the speed (the control group).

A week later, subjects were asked further questions (they were not shown the film again) and the critical one was 'Did you see any broken glass?'. In fact, there was no broken glass in the film but 16 out of 50 in the 'smashed' condition recalled seeing broken glass, seven out of 50 in the 'hit' condition and six out of 50 in the control group.

What does this mean?

This supports the argument that leading questions may cause an actual distortion in someone's memory of an event. The verb 'smashed' in a question about speed led to more participants saying 'yes' to the question 'Did you see any broken glass?' when it was asked a week later.

Loftus and Palmer suggest that this is because the verb 'smashed' distorts the memory of the event towards being more severe. This means that when participants are asked if they saw any broken glass, they are more likely to say 'yes' because broken glass fits with the modified image they have of the event.

FOR CONSIDERATION

'Over time, the information from these two sources may be integrated in such a way that we are unable to tell from which source some specific detail is recalled. All we have is one memory.' (Loftus and Palmer, 1974)

WHAT ARE THE STUDY'S CONCLUSIONS?

Loftus and Palmer suggest that there are two types of information which make up memory of a complex event: the information that we get from *perceiving* the event and the information that we get *after* the event. In this case, this was the information suggested by the questions. They concluded that the questions actually altered people's memories.

THINKING LIKE A PSYCHOLOGIST – EVALUATING THE CORE STUDY

WHAT ARE THE STRENGTHS AND WEAKNESSES OF LOFTUS AND PALMER'S METHOD?

The method used in the study was **laboratory experiments**. Loftus and Palmer manipulated the words used in the questions and measured the effect of this on recall. They did this in **controlled conditions**, keeping as many other variables as possible the same, thus allowing them to conclude that it was the words used in the questions that caused the differences in recall. This illustrates one of the major strengths of laboratory experiments – control. The more variables you have control over, the easier it becomes to draw conclusions about the effect of the individual variable on the dependent variable.

However, laboratory experiments have several weaknesses. The high level of control usually means that an artificial situation is created which makes it difficult to apply the results to everyday life. This is referred to as **low ecological validity** (see below). Participants know that they are taking part in a laboratory experiment and this will affect their behaviour in a number of ways. They will be looking for clues as to how to behave (**demand characteristics**) and they will usually want to help the experimenters by giving them the results that they think they want. Demand characteristics may have had a major effect on the results of Loftus and Palmer's first study.

WHAT TYPE OF DATA WAS COLLECTED?

Loftus and Palmer only collected **quantitative data**, that is, speed estimates and numbers of people saying that they had seen a broken headlight. Quantitative data are very useful for making comparisons and they allow statistical analysis to be conducted, but they are fairly superficial. They do not tell us anything about why people gave the answers that they did.

IS THE RESEARCH ECOLOGICALLY VALID?

There are many differences between observing an event like a car crash in real life and observing one on a television screen as part of an experiment. Some of these differences include the following:
- In an experiment, you are expecting something to happen and may be paying more attention to what is going on.
- The event is likely to be far less distressing on film than it would be in real life. This may affect your memory of the event.
- In an experiment, you may well expect to be asked questions about what you are watching and this may make you pay attention to the film in a different way.

CD-ROM

The Cognitive Approach:
Free recall v. recognition

FOR CONSIDERATION

How else could eye-witness testimony be investigated? What strengths and weaknesses might your suggested studies have?

FOR CONSIDERATION

What qualitative data could have been collected?

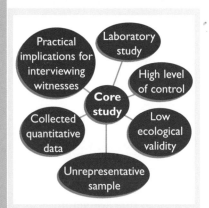

Fig. 2.5 Evaluating the core study

- What other differences can you think of between watching a car crash on television and seeing one in real life?
- How could you improve the ecological validity of this study?
- Would you expect samples of police officers or taxi drivers to give the same results?

> Did you see the defendant smash the window?

Fig. 2.6 Do not ask leading questions

You should be able to:
- describe the aim, method, sample, results and conclusions of this core study
- describe at least one alternative way in which eye-witness testimony could be investigated.

- What other factors might influence someone's memory of an event? Design a study to test the effect of one of these factors.
- What advice would you give to someone who was going to interview a witness to a hold-up in a bank?
- Describe one different sample that could be used for this study and suggest how this might affect the results.

- In real life, there may be consequences arising from the answers that you give and this may put pressure on the witness.

Overall, we can probably conclude that this laboratory experiment had low ecological validity and thus may not tell us very much about how people's memories are affected by leading questions in real life.

WAS THE SAMPLE REPRESENTATIVE?

Loftus and Palmer used student participants in both of the studies. It may be that students are not representative of the general population and therefore it may be difficult to generalise from the results of this study. Some differences between students and the general population may include the following:
- Students will usually be young and it is possible that people's memories are better when they are young.
- Students are used to taking in lots of information and then being asked questions about it. People who have not studied for many years may be less used to this.
- Students may be less experienced drivers than the general population and may be less confident in their ability to estimate speed. This may have led them to be more swayed by the words in the questions.

Students may be more susceptible to demand characteristics especially if they are students of the researchers conducting the research.

IS THE RESEARCH USEFUL?

Given that it has just been argued that the study had an **unrepresentative sample** and low ecological validity, you might feel that it was not very useful. However, despite the points made above, it is possible to identify a number of practical applications that arise from Loftus and Palmer's research. The conclusion that leading questions can affect memory has important implications for interviewing witnesses, both by police immediately or soon after an event and also by lawyers in court some time later. Interviewers should avoid leading questions and should be careful to word questions in ways that do not suggest an answer to the person that they are interviewing.

DEREGOWSKI (1972): BACKGROUND

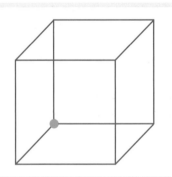

Fig. 2.7 What are you looking at?

WHAT IS PERCEPTION?

Psychologists distinguish between the **physiological process of seeing** and the **psychological process of perceiving**. Assuming that we do not have any problems with our eyesight, we need simply to open our eyes to see. Perceiving, on the other hand, involves making sense of what we are seeing and there are as many factors that affect our perception as there are factors which affect our memory (see previous study).

Fig 2.7 shows two **visual illusions** and although most of the perceptual world is not like this, the study of illusions can tell us a great deal about how the perceptual process works. If you look at the Necker cube (Fig. 2.7) for around 30 seconds, you may experience something strange. The cube appears to 'flip' so that the top appears to be in a different place. This tells us two very important things about perception:

- We automatically interpret the two-dimensional (2D) picture of a cube as if it were a three-dimensional (3D) object. We do this because we use certain cues to depth, or perspective, that are part of the drawing. This is a very important point because in the core study we are about the consider, there is evidence that such cues are learned and other cultures do not use the same cues in interpreting pictures. Remember, this is not a cube but a flat (2D) image on a piece of paper. It does not have depth and it is only the way we have learned to interpret certain cues that gives it depth. Interestingly, once we are familiar with depth cues in drawings we are unable to ignore them. Asking you to look at this cube simply as a pattern of lines on the page would be like asking you to look at but not read the title of this book!

- There are two possible interpretations to this picture. When we look at it, we are not able to decide which 'orientation' is the correct one and so the image appears to flip backwards and forwards while we attempt to decide between the two alternatives. The same process happens when you look at the image of the woman in Fig. 2.7, although it may take you a little longer to see the two alternatives. Once you have identified that this picture may be a young woman or an old woman, you can experience the same 'flipping' effect.

WHAT OTHER FACTORS INFLUENCE OUR PERCEPTION?

There are numerous other factors which have been identified by psychologists – there isn't space here to discuss them all! One interesting way in which perception has been explained is the idea of **perceptual set**.

FOR CONSIDERATION

What other factors can you think of that might influence someone's perception?

The following factors affect our perceptual set:

- **Motivation** – for example, when we are hungry we will perceive pictures of food as more attractive than when we are not hungry.
- **Emotion** – McGinnies (1949) showed that words presented subliminally (for such short times that we do not become consciously aware of them) took longer to respond to if they were unpleasant in some way.
- **Beliefs** – people who believe in UFOs are more likely to perceive an unclear figure in the sky as suspicious than people who do not believe in UFOs!

WHY STUDY OTHER CULTURES?

The use of cross-cultural studies in psychological research may help us decide which perceptual skills are **innate** and which are learned.

If we find consistent differences between the perceptual skills of different cultures, this would be evidence for the role of learning and experience in the development of perception. There have been many studies which have identified differences, for example:

- Murray Islanders were less susceptible to the Muller-Lyer illusion than English people were (Rivers,1901) (see Fig. 2.8)
- children living in rural parts of Tonga were less susceptible to the Ames room distortion than children in urban areas of the same country (Stewart, 1973) (see Fig. 2.9).

What conclusions have been drawn from cross-cultural research?

Segall (1963) concludes that it is the **environment** which affects the way we perceive. If you think about the world in which you live, you will realise that it is full of straight lines and right angles. Segall describes this as a **'carpentered environment'**. When we look at illusions such as the ones described above, we are using our past experiences of the world to help us make sense of what we are seeing. Thus the Muller-Lyer illusion and the Ames room distortion 'deceive' us because we use the angles as cues to depth. If we lived in non-carpentered environments, we would not be used to using these cues to suggest depth and hence would not be susceptible to these illusions.

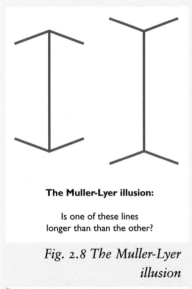

The Muller-Lyer illusion:

Is one of these lines longer than than the other?

Fig. 2.8 The Muller-Lyer illusion

Fig. 2.9 The Ames room

WHAT ABOUT PICTURES?

The core study by Deregowski reviews evidence about the perception of pictures and asks whether pictures are perceived in the same ways in all cultures. Given what we have considered so far, it is appropriate to assume that the way we draw and interpret pictures in the western world is so affected by our experiences in a carpentered world that the cues used in such pictures may not be familiar to people living in very different environments.

DEREGOWSKI (1972): THE CORE STUDY

WHAT WAS THE AIM OF THE STUDY?

The aim of the study was to review cross-cultural research into the perception of pictures with a view to answering the question 'Do pictures offer us a *lingua franca* for **inter-cultural communication**?'. In other words, do people in all cultures perceive pictures in the same way, and if they do, can we regard pictures as a universal language?

The study includes **anecdotal reports** from missionaries who describe experiences in Africa between 80 and 100 years ago. One report describes the inability of people in Nyasaland (Malawi) to interpret black and white pictures and another describes how an elderly African woman disliked a profile picture as it had only one eye. Both reports suggest that western-style pictures were a new experience for these people and that they experienced difficulties in interpreting them at first. One anecdote reported by Deregowski offers a very different view. When people were shown an image of an elephant projected on to a sheet, they reacted immediately as if the elephant were real.

Deregowski points out that this evidence is ambiguous: it suggests the need for learning to interpret western-style pictures, but it also suggests that pictorial recognition is largely independent of learning.

REVIEWS OF EXPERIMENTAL RESEARCH

Deregowski reviewed a number of pieces of experimental work conducted by Hudson. In one of these experiments, Hudson used the elephant/antelope picture shown in Figure 2.10.

The picture contains three depth cues. These are:
- **familiar size** – if larger objects are drawn very small, this would suggest that they are further away
- **overlap** – portions of nearer objects overlap and obscure portions of objects that are further away
- **perspective** – convergence of lines known to be parallel suggests distance.

Hudson's picture was shown to a variety of groups of people across Africa. The results are clear: both children and adults found it difficult to perceive depth in the picture (they were not able to explain that the hunter is pointing his spear at the antelope because the tip of the spear is actually closer to the elephant in the picture).

This finding was also confirmed in another test where participants were shown a drawing of two squares, one behind the other and connected

Fig. 2.10 Elephant/antelope picture used by Hudson

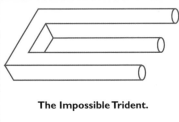

The Impossible Trident.

How many prongs are there?
Cover end of the trident and count.

Fig. 2.11 Close the book and try to copy this figure

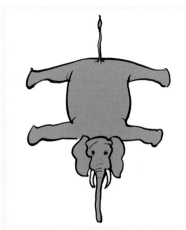

Fig. 2.12 A split-style elephant!

by a single rod, and asked to build a model of what they saw. 3D perceivers tended to build 3D models and 2D perceivers tended to build flat models.

In another test, Zambian school children were divided into 2D or 3D perceivers. They were then asked to copy a picture of the 'impossible trident' (see Fig. 2.11). The hypothesis for this experiment was that children who were 3D perceivers would be confused by the image and find it very difficult to copy but the 2D perceivers would find copying much easier. This is basically what was found.

WHAT OTHER TYPES OF PICTURE ARE THERE?

If people are not used to perspective-style pictures, they will tend to prefer the type of picture that depicts all the essential characteristics of the object even if all of these could not be seen from one viewpoint. These are referred to as **split-style drawings**.

Hudson found that both African adults and children preferred a split-style drawing of an elephant (see Fig. 2.12) over a drawing of an elephant seen from above.

This preference for split-style drawings can be seen in the artistic styles of certain cultures (such as the art of the native American Indians and that found in cave paintings in the Sahara and primitive art found in Siberia and New Zealand).

Deregowski suggests that all children have a preference for split-style drawings and that in most societies this preference is suppressed because the drawings do not convey information as accurately as perspective ones do, but in other cultures, the split-style drawing has been developed to a high artistic level. This might happen particularly if the pictures were never meant as a means of communication but were intended primarily as ornaments and include symbolic elements that enable the viewer to interpret them.

WHAT ARE THE STUDY'S CONCLUSIONS?

Deregowski concludes that pictures are not a *lingua franca* as they are not perceived in the same way in all cultures.

THINKING LIKE A PSYCHOLOGIST – EVALUATING THE CORE STUDY

WHAT ARE THE STRENGTHS AND WEAKNESSES OF DEREGOWSKI'S METHOD?

This is a complex question to answer as there are so many different aspects to the article. We will start by considering the strengths and weaknesses of Deregowski's review. Review articles are very useful as the author brings together several pieces of research and draws some general conclusions from them. Often, authors of reviews are also evaluating the research conducted by others and again this makes them valuable sources of information about the strengths and weaknesses of the original research. However, Deregowski has not conducted the research he is writing about and may be misrepresenting or misunderstanding the research he is discussing. For example, Banyard (1996) suggests that Deregowski may be slightly inaccurate in his reporting of the results from the elephant/antelope picture.

The review also contains some **anecdotal evidence** and this will lack the objectivity of controlled research. These reports came from missionaries working in Africa around 100 years ago and some of the **ethnocentric** nature of their attitudes is evident in the quotes included by Deregowski. Ethnocentrism is discussed further below. There are no references given for these anecdotes and so we cannot research them further; in some cases, they lack detail and it would be useful to know more about the event that they are describing. What exactly was flashed on to the sheet? Was it a picture or a photograph? If it was a picture, how detailed was it?

WHAT TYPE OF DATA WAS COLLECTED?

The research conducted by Hudson collected **quantitative** data, that is, numbers of people who were or were not able to perceive depth cues in pictures. However, some of the anecdotal evidence is **qualitative**, that is, it simply describes experience in words.

IS THE RESEARCH ETHNOCENTRIC?

The research described by Deregowski is ethnocentric in the way that it refers to people of other cultures as being less developed in their ability to perceive pictures. The researchers appear to be failing to consider that for many of their subjects this would have been the first time they had seen western-style drawings.

Cross-cultural research is often ethnocentric, as researchers are so used to their own cultures that it is difficult for them to be objective about a

KEY DEFINITION

ETHNOCENTRISM
The tendency to judge people by the norms and standards of your own cultural group.

ANECDOTE
An account of an incident.

FOR CONSIDERATION

Imagine a large hologram of an elephant being projected in front of you. You might react in the same way as the people, described by Deregowski, did to the picture flashed on the sheet!

KEY CONCEPT

The core study by Gould also raises these issues – see page 130.

FOR CONSIDERATION

What do you think the consequences of conducting ethnocentric research might be?

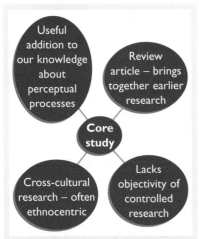

Fig. 2.13 Evaluating the core study

HOT EXAM HINTS

You should be able to:
- describe the aim of Deregowski's review and the conclusions that he reaches
- descibe the aim, method, results and conclusions of the research reviewed by Deregowski and conducted by Hudson
- explain the concept of ethnocentrism and relate it to this review.

FOR CONSIDERATION

- What advice would you give someone who was going to conduct a piece of cross-cultural research?
- Could research like this increase ethnocentric attitudes?
- Could research like this challenge ethnocentric attitudes?
- Think about cartoons! Would such images be perceived in the same way in all cultures? What other images might be difficult for people from other cultures to interpret?

different culture. It is highly likely that they will interpret what they are seeing in relation to the norms and values of their own culture. This can also affect the way that research is conducted. Some of the subjects used in Hudson's research may have been seeing paper for the first time, or asked to use a pen and paper for the first time. They will have had no previous experience of these types of tasks and it is unlikely that they would have understood the purpose of the research. There may also be ethical issues raised by such research, such as informed consent.

WHAT DOES THE STUDY TELL US ABOUT THE NATURE-NURTURE DEBATE?

Perception of pictures is not an innate skill. Rather, it is the result of learning and experience. Someone growing up in a carpentered environment will easily pick up on depth cues in pictures, but for those people who live in very different environments, these cues are meaningless. This is a very important conclusion as it not only suggests that pictures are not a *lingua franca* for inter-cultural communication but reveals the extent to which our perceptual abilities are learned ones.

IS THE STUDY USEFUL?

In the sense that we can draw the conclusions outlined above, this review may be considered to be a useful addition to our knowledge about perceptual processes. The review also highlights the dangers of ethnocentrism, particularly when conducting cross-cultural research. However, it is possible to go further than that and suggest some practical applications that arise from the review. If pictures or images are to be used cross culturally, then it is important that they are designed in ways which will be understood in the same way in all cultures.

| # BARON-COHEN, LESLIE AND FRITH (1985): BACKGROUND

WHAT IS AUTISM?

Childhood autism is a **severe developmental disorder** which affects the social functioning of individuals.

Autistic individuals are described as having a triad (three) of impairments:

1 **Impairments in social interaction**. Autistic individuals have difficulties in forming relationships and may appear aloof and indifferent to other people. They show very different non-verbal behaviours to non-autistic people, such as not making eye contact. As children, they tend not to develop pretend play or any other imaginative games and do not develop the 'turn-taking' abilities of non-autistic children. It has been suggested that an inability to empathise (imagine the thoughts and feelings of others) may be at the root of these social impairments.

2 **Impairments in communication**. Autistic individuals have difficulties with both verbal and non-verbal communication. They tend not to develop language in the same way as non-autistic people and may simply have a set of phrases or sentences that they use repeatedly. They generally do not understand the meaning of gestures, facial expressions or tone of voice. Their lack of spontaneous or make-believe play is also connected to their difficulties in communicating.

3 **Repetitive and stereotyped patterns of behaviour**. Autistic individuals often have rigid and inflexible routines which must be followed strictly. This might include the order in which daily tasks must be completed and may also include repetitive and ritualised mannerisms. Attempts to alter the routines of autistic individuals can lead to high levels of distress.

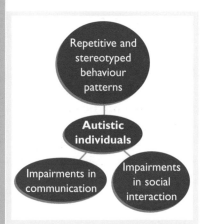

Fig. 2.14 Autistic individuals have a triad of impairments

HOW MANY PEOPLE HAVE AUTISM?

The term 'autism' is now generally used to describe a wide spectrum of disorders from **Asperger's syndrome** at one end through to individuals showing severe forms of the above impairments at the other extreme.

In 1979, Wing and Gould estimated that the incidence of autistic spectrum disorders was around 20 in 10,000. In 1997, Wing revised this estimate to suggest that the figure is now nine per 1000. Mitchell (1997) suggests that the figure is one or two per 1000 and notes that autism in boys is five times the level of autism in girls. A recent Medical Research Council report stated that one in every 166 children under 8 years is affected and the National Autistic Society recently revised its estimate from one in every 110 children to an incredible one

Fig. 2.15 A controversial theory: Is there a link between the MMR vaccine and the development of autism?

Fig. 2.16   The film Rain Man *stars Dustin Hoffman as Raymond, an autistic man with Kanner's syndrome.*

in 86, roughly double the figures suggested by the Medical Research Council. Whatever the figures are, they are certainly rising, but whether this is due to a rise in the incidence of autism or simply better diagnosis is unclear.

WHAT CAUSES AUTISM?

There have been many theories suggested for the causes of autism. Kanner originally suggested cold and uncaring parenting styles ('refrigerator' parenting) although this has been discounted. There is some evidence for a genetic component to autism supported by the fact that siblings of autistic children are far more likely to develop autism than siblings of non-autistic children (some studies suggest the risk here is as high as one in 16) and some suggestions that around one-third of parents of autistic children show some autistic tendencies (Piven and Folstein, 1994). The most recent and controversial theory suggests a link between the MMR vaccine and the development of autism.

WHAT IS THEORY OF MIND?

A recent development in the understanding of autism is the notion of **theory of mind**.

Autistic individuals are sometimes described as suffering from '**mind-blindness**' as they appear to be unable to 'read minds'. The ability to 'read minds' or to make inferences about what other people believe to be the case in any given situation allows us to predict what they will do. Clearly, lacking this basic ability would make social interaction very difficult indeed and the absence of a theory of mind would explain the **core deficits** of autism described above.

BARON-COHEN, LESLIE AND FRITH (1985): THE CORE STUDY

WHAT WAS THE AIM OF THE STUDY?

The study was designed to test the hypothesis that autistic children lack a theory of mind. The researchers state in their introduction that it is necessary to consider the cognitive functioning of autistic children 'independently of IQ' and so they use two comparison groups which are comprised of clinically normal children and children with Down's syndrome.

Baron-Cohen *et al.* use a technique originally designed by Wimmer and Perner (1983) which is referred to as the **Sally-Anne task** (see below).

WHO WERE THE PARTICIPANTS?

There were three groups of participants:

- Twenty autistic children aged 6–16 years (mean age 11 years and 11 months). Their non-verbal mental age was between 5 years and 4 months and 15 years and 9 months, with a mean of 9 years and 3 months, and their verbal mental age was between 2 years and 8 months and 7 years and 5 months, with a mean of 5 years and 5 months.
- Fourteen Down's syndrome children aged between 6 years and 3 months and 17 years, with a mean of 10 years and 11 months. Their non-verbal mental age was between 4 years and 9 months and 8 years and 6 months, with a mean of 5 years and 11 months, and their verbal mental age was between 1 year and 8 months and 4 years, with a mean of 2 years and 11 months.
- Twenty-seven clinically normal children aged between 3 years and 5 months and 5 years and 9 months. It was assumed that their verbal and non-verbal mental ages would be equivalent to their chronological age.

WHAT IS THE SALLY-ANNE TASK?

This scenario is acted out for the children using two dolls:

KEY DEFINITION

DOWN'S SYNDROME
A chromosomal disorder which is characterised by extremely low IQ but normal social functioning.

The researchers included the group of Down's syndrome children so that they could investigate the link between IQ and theory of mind. If Down's syndrome children have a theory of mind, this would mean that it does not depend on intelligence.

FOR CONSIDERATION

Produce a simple table showing the mean chronological and verbal ages of the children who participated in the research.

Fig. 2.17 The Sally-Anne task

1 The child is told which doll is Sally and which doll is Anne. The **naming question** ('Which doll is which?') is asked to ensure that children know the difference.
2 Sally places a marble in her basket and leaves. Anne takes the marble and places it in her box. Sally returns. The **critical belief question** is asked ('Where will Sally look for her marble?'). If the child points to the basket (where Sally put the marble), they pass this question as they have correctly attributed a false belief to Sally. If they point to the box, they fail this question because they have not taken into account Sally's belief about the whereabouts of the marble.
3 The **reality question** is asked ('Where is the marble really?').
4 The **memory question** is asked ('Where was the marble in the beginning?'). These two questions are asked to ensure the child has understood the scenario and to check that they haven't simply guessed the answer to the critical question.
5 The whole task is repeated using a different new location for the marble (the experimenter's pocket) so that there are now three different possible locations for the child to choose in answer to the questions.

WHAT WERE THE RESULTS?

All participants answered the naming question, the reality question and the memory question accurately.

The difference between the responses of the autistic children and the other two groups was statistically significant. The 16 autistic children that answered the question incorrectly all pointed to where the marble really was rather than where Sally originally left the marble. There were no significant differences between these autistic children and the other autistic children in terms of chronological or mental age and there were autistic children with higher mental ages who gave incorrect answers.

The fact that every single child answered the control questions correctly led the authors to conclude that they had all followed the sequence of events, that is, they understood that the marble had been moved from its original location to somewhere else. Down's syndrome and clinically normal children were able to appreciate that Sally did not know this and that she would look for her marble where she left it. They were able to respond on the basis of the doll's belief.

However, the autistic children consistently pointed to where the marble actually was (no child was ever wrong here, no one ever pointed to the box on a repeat trial when the marble was moved to the experimenter's pocket).

WHAT ARE THE STUDY'S CONCLUSIONS?

Baron-Cohen *et al.* therefore conclude that the autistic children did not appreciate the difference between their own and the doll's knowledge. They describe this as an inability to represent mental states, making them unable to attribute beliefs to others and therefore unable to predict the behaviour of others. They also conclude that neither age nor intelligence are related to theory of mind.

☕ FOR CONSIDERATION

BELIEF QUESTION
- Twenty-three out of 27 clinically normal children answered the belief question correctly on both trials.
- Twelve out of 14 Down's syndrome children answered the belief question correctly on both trials (and one child answered incorrectly on the first trial and correctly on the second trial).
- Four out of 20 autistic children answered the belief question correctly on both trials.

Fig. 2.18 The autistic children always pointed to where the marble actually was

THINKING LIKE A PSYCHOLOGIST – EVALUATING THE CORE STUDY

WHAT ARE THE STRENGTHS AND WEAKNESSES OF BARON-COHEN ET AL.'S METHOD?

The study used a **quasi-experimental design**, where the researcher does not have control over the independent variable but takes advantage of conditions where the different conditions of the independent variable occur naturally. In this study, the researchers could not randomly allocate people to the three groups but had to find autistic, Down's syndrome and developmentally normal children who were able to take part in the research.

Quasi-experimental designs are useful as they allow researchers to investigate naturally occurring variables that cannot be manipulated experimentally, but they lack some of the control of laboratory experiments. It is possible that there are other differences between the groups of participants which are unrelated to the variables being studied.

WHAT TYPE OF DATA WAS COLLECTED?

The data are **quantitative** as they are simply numbers of children that answered the belief question correctly. These are appropriate data to collect in this study as the researchers were simply proposing that more autistic children would answer this question incorrectly. However, it would have been possible to explore the children's answers further (perhaps with some open-ended questions such as 'Why will Sally look there?') which would generate qualitative data. However, this would depend on the language skills of the children being tested.

IS THE STUDY ECOLOGICALLY VALID?

It is possible to criticise the ecological validity of the study in one important respect. In everyday life, we do not attribute thoughts and beliefs to dolls but to other people. Why did the researchers choose to explore theory of mind in this way? If autistic children cannot attribute beliefs to dolls, this does not necessarily mean that they cannot attribute beliefs to people. However, Leslie and Frith (1988) replicated (repeated) the procedure used in the Sally-Anne task with real people and found similar results, suggesting that the Sally-Anne task is a valid one and can be generalised to attributing beliefs to other people.

The use of dolls may be criticised in other ways. Some of the children in this study were 11 years old or more and if the figures quoted earlier are correct, the majority of the autistic children are likely to have been

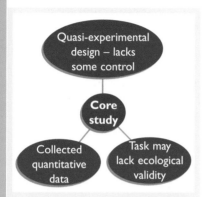

Fig. 2.19 *Evaluating the core study*

Fig. 2.20 *Playing with dolls may not be an appropriate task to give an 11-year-old boy*

boys. It may be that 'playing with dolls' is not a particularly appropriate task for these children. It can also be argued that using real people in this task is more appropriate than using dolls, particularly with autistic children who are highly unlikely to play with dolls usually.

ARE THE RESULTS USEFUL?

There are several points to make here. Firstly, there are four autistic children from the sample of 20 who did answer the belief question correctly. This slightly weakens the conclusion drawn by the researchers that autistic children lack a theory of mind. It might be more accurate to say that *most* autistic children lack a theory of mind. A more detailed study of the children who did demonstrate theory of mind might be useful. If they have this ability and are still demonstrating the triad of impairments outlined earlier, then the lack of theory of mind cannot be the 'crucial ingredient' for autism that has been suggested.

On a more positive note, there is no doubt that a lack of theory of mind is common in autistic individuals. Now that this has been established, it may be possible to develop teaching methods that attempt to encourage theory of mind skills in autistic individuals. For example, many autistic children are unable to recognise emotions from facial expressions in the same way that non-autistic individuals do (this is another manifestation of lacking a theory of mind) but can learn to interpret expressions with practice.

GARDNER AND GARDNER (1969): BACKGROUND

WHAT IS LANGUAGE?

REINFORCEMENT
A very young child will be given a drink if they point to a cup and make a sound a bit like 'drink', but an older child will have to say this much more clearly and eventually ask 'Please may I have a drink?' before the reward is given.

Fig. 2.21 Asking for a drink

Fig. 2.22 B F Skinner

 KEY CONCEPT

Some autistic children only produce sentences that they have heard before, often with the same inflexions and accents of the original speaker.

The most often quoted definition of language comes from Brown (1965) who states that language is:

> 'an arbitrary set of symbols, which, taken together, make it possible for a creature with limited powers of discrimination and a limited memory to transmit and understand an infinite variety of messages'.

In other words, Brown is saying that language is made up of **symbols** (sounds and words) which we learn have meanings and which we also learn can be combined in infinite ways to produce an infinite number of sentences. The rules are called **grammar** and most people appear to learn these rules very easily.

HOW DO CHILDREN LEARN LANGUAGE?

There have been two major approaches to explaining how children learn language and these are summarised below.

The learning theory approach

This approach has been mainly the work of **Skinner** and uses the concepts of **operant conditioning** theory to explain the learning (or acquisition) of language and all other behaviours. Skinner starts with an infant's babbling. When infants babble they produce a whole range of sounds, some of which will sound a little like words (such as da-da). When this happens the child's carers will reward this by getting very excited and giving the infant a lot of praise and attention. This is termed **positive reinforcement**. They will also probably repeat the word as it is meant to be said, thus encouraging the child to imitate the sound. As the child's language skills improve they will be shaped, as the carer will first reward sounds that are only vaguely like a word but will gradually expect the word to be produced more and more accurately before rewarding. The same process will explain the move from one-word utterances to sentences.

These processes are no doubt involved in the acquisition of language, but critics of Skinner have raised several important issues. Firstly, it is not clear how these relatively slow processes can explain the very rapid rate of language acquisition in the first few years of life. Secondly, critics have argued that these processes do not fully explain the learning of language rules as carers will often reward a child when the meaning of their utterance is clear even though the syntax may be incorrect. Finally, Skinner's theory does not explain the incredibly creative nature of language.

Language Acquisition Device

The second major explanation of language acquisition comes from **Chomsky**. While accepting that the processes outlined above must play a part in language acquisition, Chomsky proposes that we must have some form of innate (inborn) ability to acquire and produce language. He proposes that children have an innate **Language Acquisition Device (LAD)** which equips them with the skills they need to develop language. There is evidence to support the notion that we have some innate understanding of the **deep structure** of language, including the fact that all languages share some characteristics (language rules) and that the spontaneous emergence of gestural language in deaf children shows the characteristics of language such as verbs, nouns and syntax.

IS LANGUAGE UNIQUE TO HUMANS?

Chomsky would argue that only humans have the Language Acquisition Device described above. Other theorists such as Lenneberg support this claiming that there is no evidence that non-human animals can learn language. Such arguments assume *a difference between language and communication* and claim that while animals can communicate in complex ways, they do not have the ability to produce infinite numbers of new utterances (creativity) or to demonstrate understanding of the grammatical rules of language.

Some of the most exciting research in this area has been the attempts to teach chimpanzees to use language. Early attempts, such as those by the Kellogs failed because they were attempting to teach chimpanzees to use spoken language. It became evident that chimpanzees simply do not have the vocal apparatus required to produce speech sounds, but does this mean that they cannot learn to use other forms of language? The core study in the next section was the first attempt to teach a chimpanzee to use American Sign Language. It was conducted by Allan and Trixie Gardner, a husband and wife team working at the University of Nevada.

GARDNER AND GARDNER (1969): THE CORE STUDY

WHAT WAS THE AIM OF THE STUDY?

The study aimed to see if it was possible to teach a chimpanzee to use a human language. The researchers decided to use a sign language – **American Sign Language (ASL)** or **Ameslan** – as it had previously been shown that chimpanzees could not make all the correct speech sounds necessary for spoken language but that they make a number of gestures naturally and have been shown to develop more while in captivity (begging, etc.).

WHO WAS TAUGHT SIGN LANGUAGE?

The researchers chose a chimpanzee as this species is among the most intelligent of animals and perhaps, more importantly, they are highly sociable and have formed strong attachments to human beings. The researchers emphasise this as they argue that social relationships are crucial for the formation of language in humans and so it was a primary consideration in the choice of animal.

Washoe lived with a number of human companions (the research team) and was with someone all the time. The researchers used only ASL in her presence, although there was obviously occasionally a need for some spoken English between researchers and other personnel. The rule was that sounds could be made (laughing, clapping, etc.), but they should be sounds that Washoe could imitate.

Fig. 2.23 Washoe was a wild, caught chimpanzee who was estimated to be between 8 and 14 months at the start of the experiment. This is very young for a chimpanzee as they are completely dependent until at least 2 years old, semi-dependent until 4 and the first signs of sexual maturity appear at around the age of 8. They are fully grown at between 12 and 16 and can live for 40 years or more.

HOW WAS WASHOE TAUGHT TO USE SIGN LANGUAGE?

Previous researchers had already commented on the **imitative powers** of chimpanzees for any non-verbal behaviours. The Gardners used **imitation** as a training method by making the correct signs to Washoe and repeating these until she made the correct sign herself. Correct signs were **reinforced** or rewarded, usually with food or tickles! Signs were also 'shaped' by the researchers repeating the sign correctly for Washoe until she repeated it herself more accurately.

WHAT DID WASHOE LEARN?

Initially, complete records of Washoe's signing behaviour were made, but as her signing increased this became an impossible task. During the sixteenth month of the study a new procedure was agreed.

When a new sign was introduced the researchers waited until three different observers had observed the sign being used spontaneously (with no prompting) and in an appropriate context. The sign was then

Signs used by Washoe within 22 months of the beginning of training (in order of appearance):

Come-gimme	flower
more	cover-blanket
up	*dog
sweet	you
open	napkin/bib
tickle	in
go	brush
out	hat
hurry	*I-me
hear-listen	shoes
toothbrush	*smell
drink	pants
hurt	clothes
sorry	cat
funny	key
please	baby
food-eat	*clean

* These signs did not meet the stringent criteria set by the researchers but were observed on more than half the days in a 30-day period. Strictly, this means 30 signs were learned during the first 22 months.

added to a checklist in which its occurrence and context were recorded. To count as learned a sign had to appear at least once a day over a period of 15 consecutive days.

Thirty signs met this criteria by the end of the twenty-second month. A further four signs were judged to be learned despite not being observed on 15 consecutive days (they did appear at least once a day on 15 out of 30 consecutive days).

Washoe learned four signs in the first seven months, nine signs in the second seven months and 21 new signs in the third seven months. During the final month covered by the study Washoe used a minimum of 23 signs every day.

WHAT LANGUAGE SKILLS DOES WASHOE HAVE?

Washoe has learned **differentiation** – she started using the sign for flower for the smell of tobacco or cooking smells and so the researchers introduced the sign for smell. Gradually, she learned to use the two signs flower and smell appropriately, although sometimes she still uses flower when smell would be more appropriate.

Washoe can **transfer** signs – more and open were taught in very specific contexts but have transferred to other contexts. This transfer has also happened with dog (to barking) and key (from a specific small padlock key to any key or lock).

Washoe uses **two- and three-sign combinations** which she has generated herself such as 'gimme tickle' (signed before the researchers had ever asked her to tickle one of them) and 'open food drink' when asking for the refrigerator to be opened. Other examples of combinations include 'please open hurry' and 'gimme drink please'.

WHAT ARE THE STUDY'S CONCLUSIONS?

The Gardners conclude that their study has demonstrated that sign language is an **appropriate medium** for teaching to the chimpanzee. They suggest that the fact that Washoe can transfer signs and can combine signs is evidence that she will go on to develop more language skills. They dismiss the question of whether Washoe has learned a language or not by arguing that this implies a distinction between one class of communicative behaviour and another, although for other researchers this remains a crucial debate.

Fig. 2.24 What Washoe learned

THINKING LIKE A PSYCHOLOGIST – EVALUATING THE CORE STUDY

WHAT ARE THE STRENGTHS AND WEAKNESSES OF GARDNER AND GARDNER'S METHOD?

This is a **case study**, that is, an in-depth study of one individual, and produces rich, detailed data. However, it is difficult to generalise from a case study as only one individual has been studied who is unlikely to be representative of the general population. For example, Washoe might have been a very clever chimpanzee who learned far more than other chimpanzees might have done, or she might have been less able than other chimpanzees. Either way, it would be wrong to draw conclusions about the language abilities of chimpanzees from the study of just one.

WHAT TYPE OF DATA WAS COLLECTED?

Data referring to the number of signs that had been learned and the number of times they were produced are **quantitative** data. The strict criteria under which these data were collected is a strength of the study as the researchers did not simply list each sign as learned when it had been shown once. However, these criteria could be criticised as being arbitrary. Why is a sign not learned if it only appears once a day for 13 days rather than 15 days?

Some of the other data are **qualitative**, such as the descriptions of Washoe using signs in different contexts. These are very valuable data in a study such as this as they add significantly to our understanding of what Washoe has learned.

WHAT DOES THE STUDY TELL US ...

About the nature-nurture debate?

The study suggests that chimpanzees are capable of learning a language, at least to a basic level. Although in her natural environment, Washoe would not spontaneously produce sign language, it is clear that she is able to adapt to new environments and learn new skills.

About reinforcement?

A **positive reinforcer** is a **positive consequence** that follows a behaviour. A reinforcer can be anything at all that makes a behaviour more likely to occur again. The study demonstrates the power of reinforcement to produce new behaviours. Washoe would not have produced signs if she did not find this reinforcing. The study suggests that reinforcement plays a crucial role in the learning of language in chimpanzees, but whether we can generalise this to humans is less clear. Reinforcement is obviously

Fig. 2.25 Evaluating the core study

FOR CONSIDERATION

Think about the reliability and validity of the criteria used by the researchers.

important while children are developing language, but as we have already seen, it is unlikely to be enough to explain the very rapid development of language that is observed in children.

IS THE STUDY ETHICAL?

Washoe was a wild, caught chimpanzee. She would have been caught and taken from her mother while she was still very dependent on her care. This would no doubt have caused extreme distress to both chimpanzees. While in the Gardners' care, she was well looked after but was denied the company of other chimpanzees which might also be considered unethical. There are now countries which would prohibit such research as they have granted the Great Apes the same rights that protect humans.

IS THE STUDY USEFUL?

Opinion is divided on this question. Direct applications are difficult to identify unless you think that the ability to communicate with animals would be useful. The usefulness of this study is evident when you look at how research like this has changed the way that we regard animals. As stated above, there are moves towards increased protection, particularly from experimentation, for all of the Great Apes and this is a direct result of the achievements of chimpanzees like Washoe.

 FOR CONSIDERATION

'If you could talk to the animals ...' what would you say?

 HOT EXAM HINTS

You should be able to:
- describe the aim, procedure and results of this study
- comment on whether you think that Washoe demonstrated language or simply some learned behaviours.

FOR CONSIDERATION

1 Was Washoe really using sign language or had she simply learned a complex set of behaviours that allowed her to get reinforcements from her 'trainers'?
2 Would there have been any experimenter bias in the study? How could this have been reduced?
3 Was the study ethical?

Fig. 2.26 Should chimpanzees be removed from the wild for the purposes of research?

USEFUL RESOURCES

STRENGTHS OF THE COGNITIVE APPROACH

- High level of control in laboratory conditions (e.g. Loftus and Palmer).
- Contributes to our understanding of nature-nurture debate (Deregowski).
- May help understand those with cognitive problems and may lead to practical applications for teaching/ treatment (e.g. Baron-Cohen).
- Increased our understanding of the cognitive abilities of other species (e.g. Gardner and Gardner).

WEAKNESSES OF THE COGNITIVE APPROACH

- Some research has low ecological validity (e.g. Loftus and Palmer).
- Tends to use quantitative rather than qualitative measures.
- Can be reductionist.

 CD-ROM

Revision: Crosswords: Cognitive

BOOKS

Gross, R. (2001) *Psychology: The Science of Mind of Behaviour*, Hodder & Stoughton, 4th edn.
This is an excellent general psychology textbook and chapters 15, 16, 17, 19, 21 and 40 will give you plenty of information on the topics covered in this section.

Moxon, D. (2000) *Memory*, Heinemann.
This is an easy-to-read book covering all the theories of memory as well as looking at eye-witness testimony in more detail.

Loftus, E. (1996) *Eye Witness Testimony*, Harvard University Press.
This is an in-depth account of Loftus' research into eye-witness testimony.

O'Connell, S. (1997) *Mind Reading: How We Learn to Love and Lie*, Arrow books.
This is a fascinating book that examines the concept of 'theory of mind' in detail and considers its significance not only for understanding the minds of autistic people but also people in general (including psychopaths) and animals.

WEBSITES

Go to www.heinemann.co.uk/hotlinks and insert the code 670XP.
Look at the websites listed under Cognitive: Useful websites.

CHAPTER 3

THE DEVELOPMENTAL APPROACH

THE CORE STUDIES

WHAT IS DEVELOPMENTAL PSYCHOLOGY?

Developmental psychology takes a 'life span' approach to psychology and considers a range of changes that occur throughout our lives. This includes the study of the development of cognitive processes such as thinking, problem solving and language and the development of social processes such as attachments to others and play. Developmental psychologists are interested in the many factors that contribute to making us the people that we are and, for this reason, have a great deal of interest in the nature-nurture debate. Developmental psychologists are also interested in development later in life, through adolescence, adulthood and into old age.

THE CORE STUDIES

Samuel and Bryant (1984)

This is an experiment, replicating an earlier piece of research conducted by Piaget. The researchers changed one part of the original procedure in order to examine its effect on the results of the study.

Bandura, Ross and Ross (1961)

This is also an experiment, conducted in controlled laboratory conditions. The researchers wanted to investigate the effects of an aggressive 'model' (that is an adult behaving aggressively) on children's behaviour. They also investigated gender differences in aggression. This study raises several ethical issues which you will need to consider.

Hodges and Tizard (1989b)

This is one report from a longitudinal study which followed a group of children who had spent the first two years of their lives in institutions. Some of these children were adopted and some were restored to their biological families. Hodges and Tizard compared these children with 'matched comparison' and investigated a number of aspects of their social relationships at age 16.

Freud (1909)

This is one of Freud's famous case studies and the only one which focused on a child. In it, Freud investigates reasons why Little Hans developed a phobia of horses and also considers evidence for the existence of the Oedipus complex.

SECTION I | SAMUEL AND BRYANT (1984): BACKGROUND

KEY CONCEPTS

- Piaget did not assume that intelligence was a fixed trait (feature) as many early intelligence theorists did, but that intelligence was a process of adapting to the environment and thus would change over time.
- Piaget suggested that children have very different intellectual (cognitive) abilities to adults and therefore see the world in very different ways. This may seem obvious to us now, but it was a new proposal at the time, and the whole field of cognitive development can be traced back to Piaget's work.

KEY DEFINITIONS

SCHEMA, *plural* **SCHEMATA**
An internal representation of a physical or mental action.

KEY CONCEPT

The process of adding new information to already existing schemata is called **assimilation**. If the schema needs to be modified in some way, this process is called **accommodation**.

Piaget's stages of cognitive development	
Stage	**Age (years)**
Sensori-motor	0–2
Pre-operational	2–7
Concrete operational	7–11
Formal operational	11+

WHAT IS COGNITIVE DEVELOPMENT?

Cognitive development refers to the development of thinking, reasoning and problem solving skills. Views on cognitive development have profound effects on the way in which society views and educates children. The traditional view stated that children's minds were 'blank slates' (*tabula rasa*) to be filled with knowledge. Children were considered to be 'miniature adults' and this approach did not recognise that children's intellectual abilities were any different from adults. A cognitive developmental view suggests that children's intellectual abilities are qualitatively different from that of adults. Children do not think about the world in the same way that adults do.

WHO WAS PIAGET?

Piaget was born in Switzerland in 1896 and trained as a zoologist. He was interested in how animals adapt to their environments and this interest broadened to include children. Piaget also worked for a time with Binet (who developed the first intelligence tests) and became fascinated by the mistakes that children make. He thought that analysing children's mistakes would be of much more value than analysing their correct answers. It was his work on intelligence tests which led him to believe that children's mistakes were not just random errors but demonstrated the way that they thought about the world, and this led to his theory of cognitive development.

HOW DOES COGNITIVE DEVELOPMENT OCCUR?

From birth, children **interact** with their environment and the information that they build up create **schemata**. For example, a baby has an innate sucking reflex, which means that they will suck anything that is put into their mouth. This schema 'works' for the infant until they come across a different sort of drinking cup or a straw and they then need to acquire some new information to make their sucking schema 'fit' their environment again.

Piaget proposed that later in childhood, children develop higher order mental abilities which allow them to interact with the world in complex ways. Piaget called these **operations**. Piaget also proposed that cognitive development takes place in stages, with the child able to perform different sorts of cognitive operations at each stage.

THE STAGES OF COGNITIVE DEVELOPMENT?

Piaget stated that all children go through four stages of cognitive development. Each stage is characterised by what cognitive tasks children can and cannot perform. He stated that all children go through these stages in the same order and at approximately the same time.

Fig. 3.1 Object permanence

Fig. 3.2 Piaget's three mountains scene

Fig. 3.3 The amount remains the same despite its change in appearance

FOR CONSIDERATION

If your teacher asked you a question and you answered and then the teacher simply repeated the question, would you think that you should give a different answer this time?

HOW DID PIAGET TEST HIS IDEAS?

Piaget conducted many studies which demonstrate the ways in which children's thinking about the world differs from adults.

Object permanence

In the sensori-motor stage, Piaget claimed that 'out of sight is out of mind'. Objects that can no longer be seen, no longer exist. Piaget demonstrated this by visibly hiding objects from babies under a cover. From 0 to 5 months, babies will not look for the object, but by 8 months they will search for it.

Centration

The thinking of children prior to the concrete operational stage is described as **egocentric** – they are unable to understand that others may think, feel and see things differently. Piaget conducted an experiment using a 3D model of a mountain. Children stood at one side of this model and had to select a photograph showing the view of the model from someone else's perspective. In the pre-operational stage, children select the photograph which shows the view that they can see.

Conservation

One of the characteristics of pre-operational stage thinking is a lack of conservation skills. Children are unable to understand that characteristics such as mass or volume remain the same despite changes in their appearance. Piaget conducted experiments where he showed children the same amount of liquid in identical sized beakers and asked them if they were the same. Then he would pour the liquid from one beaker into a shorter, fatter beaker and ask the child if they were still the same. In the pre-operational stage, children did not recognise that the amounts were still the same, but by the concrete operational stage, children are able to conserve, that is, recognise that the amount remains the same despite changes in appearance.

HAS PIAGET'S WORK BEEN CRITICISED?

There is enormous support for Piaget's theory but critics have suggested modifications to it. Some of the criticisms include the fact that Piaget may have underestimated the role of individual and social factors in cognitive development and the role played by society.

Piaget tended to use very small samples of children and less controlled experimental conditions than would be considered appropriate today. He also failed to consider the child's social understanding of the experimental condition and this is the criticism that is considered by Samuel and Bryant in their study. They suggest that Piaget's repetition of the same question in the conservation tasks may have led the child to think that they were supposed to give a different answer the second time they were asked the question. If this criticism is a valid one, it would mean that Piaget may have underestimated the children's conservation abilities.

SAMUEL AND BRYANT (1984): THE CORE STUDY

WHAT WAS THE AIM OF THE STUDY?

Samuel and Bryant are critical of the method used by Piaget in his conservation studies. They suggest that the design of the experiment encourages children to give the wrong answer simply because they are being asked the same question twice. This conclusion comes from a study cited by Samuel and Bryant in their article. Rose and Blank (1974) had investigated this hypothesis using a conservation of number task (rows of counters, initially side by side and then with one row spread out to make it appear longer) with 6-year-old children. They found that dropping the pre-transformational (first) question had a significant effect. Far more 6-year-olds were able to give the correct answer to the post-transformational (second) question.

Samuel and Bryant's study broadens these conclusions. Specifically, it widens the age groups used and it involves three different types of conservation tasks (number, mass and volume).

Fig. 3.4 Rose and Blank's conservation of number task

WHO WERE THE PARTICIPANTS?

The 252 children aged between 5 years and 8 years and 6 months who took part in the experiment were all at schools and playgroups in Devon. Four age groups were created with mean ages of 5 years and 3 months, 6 years and 3 months, 7 years and 3 months and 8 years and 3 months. Each group had 63 children and these were further subdivided into three groups of 21 children (closely matched for age) and each subgroup underwent a different condition.

WHAT WERE THE CONDITIONS?

1 Standard – the traditional two-question format.
2 One question – post-transformation question asked only.
3 Fixed array control condition – transformation not shown to the child; all they saw was the post-transformational array.

Each child was tested four times on each task (mass, number and volume). Two of these trials used equal quantities and two used unequal quantities. order of trials and materials was systematically varied between children.

WHAT WERE THE RESULTS?

There was no difference between the results for equal and unequal quantities and so the authors pooled the results. The results can be compared by age and by type of task as well as by the crucial independent variable (**questioning**).

The results are given as mean number of errors (therefore the higher the number, the worse the children did). In the table below, the results are also pooled for all four trials of the three tasks (mass, number and volume), so the maximum number of errors is 12.

Results by mean number of errors

	Standard	**One question**	**Fixed array**
5-year-olds	8.5	7.3	8.5
6-year-olds	5.7	4.3	6.4
7-year-olds	3.2	2.5	4.8
8-year-olds	1.6	1.3	3.3

Fig. 3.5 Children taking part in a conservation task

From this table, we can draw the following conclusions:

1 All ages make fewer errors on the one-question condition than the other two conditions.
2 The older children make fewer errors than the younger children.
3 The fixed array (control condition) produced the highest number of errors.

The table below looks at the effect of the different type of task. Each child had four trials with each task and so the maximum number of errors is four.

Results by effect of different type of task

	Standard	**One question**	**Fixed array**
Mass	1.5	1.2	1.7
Number	1.4	1.0	1.5
Volume	1.8	1.6	2.5

From this table, we can draw the following conclusions:

1 Children make fewer errors on the conservation of mass task and most errors on the conservation of volume task.
2 They make fewer errors on the one question task and most on the fixed array (control condition).
3 This effect is particularly strong when you look at the mean number of errors for conservation of volume in the fixed array task. Imagine being shown two very different-shaped containers with an amount of water in each. It would be very difficult to make a judgement about the quantity in each.

WHAT ARE THE STUDY'S CONCLUSIONS?

Rose and Blank's original hypothesis is *confirmed*. Children who fail the traditional conservation task do not always fail because they do not understand the principle of conservation. They fail because the repetition of 'the same question about the same material makes them think they should give a different answer the second time'.

However, the study also provides a great deal of *support* for Piaget's theory. It confirms that children do better on conservation tasks as they get older and also that the conservation of number task was easier than the other two tasks.

THINKING LIKE A PSYCHOLOGIST – EVALUATING THE CORE STUDY

WHAT ARE THE STRENGTHS AND WEAKNESSES OF SAMUEL AND BRYANT'S METHOD?

The study used an **independent measures experimental design**. The experiment had a high level of **control** as all variables, except the crucial one of questioning, were kept constant. However, experimental designs sometimes lack **ecological validity** and this is discussed in more detail below. 'Independent measures' means that different children were used in each of the three conditions. This is the most appropriate design to use to test this research question, as if the researchers had tested the same children in all three conditions there would definitely have been **order effects**.

Because there are different children in all three conditions, there is the possibility that there are individual differences between the groups of children. This is unlikely, however, as large numbers of children were tested and they were allocated randomly to the three groups.

The study is also a **replication** of previous research, although Samuel and Bryant added the two-question and the fixed array conditions to the original design. Replications are very useful in psychological research for confirming previous findings or where slight changes in methodology are used to investigate the effects of these changes.

WAS THE SAMPLE REPRESENTATIVE?

Samuel and Bryant tested 252 children which is a large **sample**. They tested children from 5–8 years which allowed them to draw conclusions about the age at which children started to be able to conserve. They all came from one area of England (Devon) which might mean that they are not representative of children from other areas of the country. For example, if Devon used different teaching strategies to other parts of the country, this might have an effect on the children's cognitive abilities. This is not really a criticism of the study, and overall the sample is large enough to allow generalisations to be made.

WHAT TYPE OF DATA WAS COLLECTED?

The data collected were **quantitative**. Samuel and Bryant only give us the numbers of errors made by the children and no other information. The advantages of this type of data is that it can be subjected to statistical analysis and allows easy comparisons between groups. The weaknesses of this type of data is that it tells us nothing about how the

Fig. 3.6 Order effects

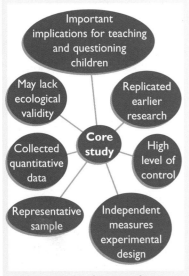

Fig. 3.7 Evaluating the core study

FOR CONSIDERATION

Suggest one way in which Samuel and Bryant could have collected qualitative data. What sort of information could they have collected?

Fig. 3.8 Asking children to choose between two beakers of juice might be a more ecologically valid method

HOT EXAM HINTS

You should be able to:
- explain why Samuel and Bryant replicated Piaget's experiment and what change they made to the procedure
- define conservation
- describe the aim, sample, method, results and conclusion of this study. (Remember that the study offers support for Piaget as well as criticising his original procedure.)

FOR CONSIDERATION

1 What change did Samuel and Bryant make to Piaget's original procedure and why did they make this change?
2 What support for Piaget is there in the results of this study?
3 Suggest one other way in which conservation skills could be investigated. Does your suggested study have high or low ecological validity?

children responded to the tasks. Did they ask any questions? Did they ever say they didn't know? Were they sure about their answers or unsure? This is the kind of information that could be illustrated by qualitative data such as quotes from the children.

IS THE STUDY ETHICAL?

The study used children under 16 years as the participants. Parental consent can only be assumed as the researchers do not give us this information. The task itself does not raise any serious ethical concerns as it is unlikely to have distressed the children in any way and no deception was used.

IS THE RESEARCH ECOLOGICALLY VALID?

This is a difficult question to answer. The task itself is quite an artificial one. It is not an everyday occurrence to ask children this type of question, although the skills that are being tested are everyday skills. Perhaps a more ecologically valid method would have been to ask children to choose which of two beakers of juice or rows of sweets they would prefer to have. This would be more 'real' to the children, as well as demonstrating clearly that they could conserve.

There are some difficulties in evaluating the actual question used as the researchers do not tell us the exact wording of the question. Asking a child 'Are they the same?' may be a slightly ambiguous question. There are many ways in which this question might have been asked and it is possible that children may have interpreted the question differently.

DOES THE STUDY GIVE AN INDIVIDUAL OR A SITUATIONAL EXPLANATION OF BEHAVIOUR?

Although this is not used in any discussion of the results, it is possible to consider the study in relation to this issue. The children's answers were not solely a result of their levels of cognitive development but were also dependent on their *understanding of the situation*. In the two-question condition, children believed that they were expected to give a different answer the second time they were asked the question (whatever it was) and this would suggest that it was the situation that determined their behaviour rather than their ability to conserve.

IS THE STUDY USEFUL?

This study has important implications for teaching children and for psychologists who question children. It clearly demonstrates that repeating questions when talking to children makes them think that they need to give a different answer. This has been demonstrated by several other researchers who have tested children's eye-witness testimony. If children are asked the same questions repeatedly, they will offer different answers to subsequent questions.

BANDURA, ROSS AND ROSS (1961): BACKGROUND

WHAT IS BEHAVIOURISM?

Behaviourism has been a highly influential approach in the development of psychology. Behaviourists argue that all behaviours can be explained in terms of **learning from the environment.**

Classical conditioning

Classical conditioning is learning by **association.** This was first demonstrated by Pavlov in his famous experiments with dogs. He showed that laboratory dogs had learned to associate the sound of a bell with being fed and that this association was so strong that the dogs would salivate when they heard a bell ringing, even though they could not smell or see any food. Classical conditioning explanations can be applied to a whole range of human reflex actions. For example, if you have learned to associate a certain food (or drink) with being ill, then you may feel ill at the sight of that food, or if you have had unpleasant experiences at the dentist, you may show fear at the sight or sound of a dentist's drill or the smell of the mouthwash you are given at the dentist.

Operant conditioning

Operant conditioning, sometimes called instrumental conditioning, is learning through the consequences of actions. There are three main consequences that behaviourists identify:

- If we do something and it has a pleasant consequence, we are more likely to produce that behaviour again. The pleasant consequence is a positive reinforcer. Almost anything can be a reinforcer.
- If we do something and it has a negative consequence (punishment), we will be less likely to produce that behaviour again.
- If we do something and it stops or prevents an unpleasant consequence such as pain or being shouted out, this is a negative reinforcer.

The above two approaches have many practical applications in education and in clinical psychology such as treatments for phobias and other disorders.

WHAT IS SOCIAL LEARNING THEORY?

Bandura *et al.* suggest that learning can also result from observing the behaviour of others and this is called **modelling.** The implication of modelling is that children learn from watching the behaviour of those around them, even when they themselves are not being directly reinforced. Many people can act as role models for children. Crucial role models can include parents, teachers, peers and siblings. This core study considers the effect of watching an adult behave aggressively.

Fig. 3.9 Pavlov's experiment into classical conditioning

KEY CONCEPT

Advertisers are aware of the power of associative learning and will design adverts that associate their products with a range of pleasant images, such as relaxing holidays or successful careers or relationships. The theory suggests that if we see this pairing often enough, we will have pleasant associations with the product and will therefore be more likely to buy it!

Fig. 3.10 Behaviourism

CD-ROM

The Developmental Approach: Classical conditioning: technical terms, and Operant conditioning: technical terms

Fig. 3.11 Will his older brother be a model for this small child?

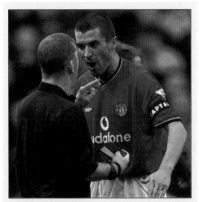

Fig. 3.12 How might observing these people affect children's behaviour?

FOR CONSIDERATION

Why were the children matched?

What practical applications does this kind of research have?

For some time, there has been concern that the behaviour of media images has an effect on children's behaviour. Gangsta rappers, footballers and soap stars are often criticised for being poor role models, the worst aspects of their behaviour being learned by the next generation. This concern has also fuelled the debate about the effects of TV violence on children's behaviour.

WHO WERE THE PARTICIPANTS?

They included 36 boys and 36 girls who all attended the Stanford University Nursery School. The children had a mean age of 4 years and 4 months (range 3 years and 1 month to 5 years and 9 months).

The study was carried out by a female experimenter, and one female and one male were the adult models.

There were eight experimental groups, each with six children and a control group of 24 children.

The eight experimental groups in Bandura et al.'s study

Group	No. of children	Sex of children	Sex of model	Aggressive/ non-aggressive model
1	6	M	M	A
2	6	M	M	N-A
3	6	M	F	A
4	6	M	F	N-A
5	6	F	M	A
6	6	F	M	N-A
7	6	F	F	A
8	6	F	F	N-A
Control	(24)			

The children were matched on the basis of their pre-existing aggressiveness, which was rated on four 5-point scales by the experimenter and a nursery school teacher before the experiment began.

WHAT IS THE CORE STUDY ABOUT?

This is an early research study into the effects of observing aggression. Children were exposed to adults acting aggressively towards toys and the children's behaviour was observed to see if they imitated the adult's behaviour. The researchers were also interested in gender differences in aggressive behaviour, and whether children were more likely to imitate same-sex models.

BANDURA, ROSS AND ROSS (1961): THE CORE STUDY

WHAT WAS THE AIM OF THE STUDY?

The study tested four hypotheses on the participants described on page 51:

1 Children exposed to an adult (the 'model') behaving aggressively towards a toy will imitate this behaviour in the absence of the model.
2 Children exposed to a non-aggressive model will show less aggressive behaviour.
3 Children will imitate same-sex models more then opposite-sex models.
4 Boys may be more pre-disposed to imitate aggressive models than girls.

KEY CONCEPT

These hypotheses are based on several assumptions:

- that children have learned imitative habits, most likely from being previously reinforced (rewarded) for imitation by parents, etc.
- that parents reward imitation of same-sex behaviour and do not reward opposite-sex behaviour, so children may be more likely to imitate same-sex models.

HOW WAS THE RESEARCH CARRIED OUT?

1 The children were brought *individually* to the experimental room and the model, who was waiting outside, was invited in. The child was taken to one area of the room with a small table and chair. Materials for potato printing and making pictures with stickers were provided. The experimenter then took the model to another corner which contained a tinker toy set, a mallet and 5-foot inflatable BoBo doll. In the non-aggressive condition, the model assembled the tinker toys and did not play with the BoBo doll at all. In the aggressive condition, the model was aggressive towards to the BoBo doll. The aggressive acts were deliberately distinctive so that imitation would be easy to identify. The model put the doll on its side, struck it with the mallet, tossed it in the air and kicked it around the room. This sequence of behaviour was repeated three times. The model was verbally aggressive and also used a number of non-aggressive phrases. After ten minutes, the child was taken to another room.

2 The final room contained a number of aggressive toys and non-aggressive toys and also a 3-foot BoBo doll. The child was in this room for 20 minutes, during which time their behaviour was rated by judges observing through a one-way mirror. Three measures of imitation were recorded: **imitation of physical aggression** (striking the BoBo doll with the mallet, punching it on the nose, sitting on the doll, kicking the doll and tossing it in the air); **imitative verbal aggression**; and **imitative non-aggressive verbal responses**. Other behaviours were also recorded: mallet aggression, i.e. striking objects other than the doll, and sitting on the doll but not being aggressive towards it. These two behaviours were recorded as partially aggressive. Non-imitative aggressive behaviours such as punching the doll, any verbally aggressive statements other than the ones made by the model and aggressive gun play were also recorded. The 20 minutes were divided up into 240 5-second intervals and the child's behaviour was recorded at each one of these 5-second intervals.

FOR CONSIDERATION

Before being tested for imitation, the children were subjected to a mild level of 'aggression arousal' to ensure that they felt aggressive. This was done by taking them to a room which contained a lot of highly attractive toys and letting the child play with them. After one or two minutes, the child was told that these were the experimenter's best toys and she had decided to keep them for some other children. The child was told that they could play with the toys in the next room.

FOR CONSIDERATION

Do you think the 'aggression arousal' stage was ethical?

WHAT WERE THE RESULTS?

Children in the aggressive condition reproduced a lot of the physical and verbal aggression used by the model, whereas children in the non-aggressive and control conditions showed virtually none of this behaviour.

Mean scores for imitative physical aggression

	Experimental groups				Control groups
	Aggressive		Non-aggressive		
	Female model	Male model	Female model	Male model	
Girls	5.5	7.2	2.5	0.0	1.2
Boys	12.4	25.8	0.2	1.5	2.0

Mean scores for imitative verbal aggression

	Experimental groups				Control groups
	Aggressive		Non-aggressive		
	Female model	Male model	Female model	Male model	
Girls	13.7	2.0	0.3	0.0	0.7
Boys	4.3	12.7	1.1	0.0	1.7

Mean scores for non-imitative aggression

	Experimental groups				Control groups
	Aggressive		Non-aggressive		
	Female model	Male model	Female model	Male model	
Girls	21.3	8.4	7.2	1.4	6.1
Boys	16.2	36.7	26.1	22.3	24.6

- Children in the aggressive condition also copied the models' non-aggressive verbal responses and none of the children in the other conditions did.

- Children who observed non-aggressive models produced far less partial imitation than the experimental and control groups and spent far more time simply sitting quietly and not playing with any of the toys.

- Some gender differences were found: boys produced more imitative physical aggression than girls, but there was no difference in imitation of verbal aggression.

THINKING LIKE A PSYCHOLOGIST – EVALUATING THE CORE STUDY

WHAT ARE THE STRENGTHS AND WEAKNESSES OF BANDURA *ET AL.*'S METHOD?

The method used was a **laboratory experiment** with **observational measures**. Laboratory experiments allow for high levels of control which are evident in the study, for example the way that the model produced exactly the same behaviour for each child and the fact that each child was observed in the same room with the same toys.

Laboratory experiments often lack **ecological validity** and you may feel that the situations that the children were put in were highly artificial and do not bear much relation to everyday life. Experiments such as these raise **ethical issues** and this is discussed further below. The children were rated by their nursery teacher and an experimenter for pre-existing levels of aggression and these ratings were used to match the children. This is another example of experimental control, although the ratings may be slightly subjective and the teacher may have known some children better than others. The children were also observed playing with the toys and the experimenters used a system of categories to code their behaviour. There may be some error or observer bias here.

In addition, all the children were observed using the same categories and there are results for 'imitative aggression' recorded for the children in the non-aggressive model condition and the control condition. Even if the children did display the behaviours shown by the aggressive model, it cannot be correct to call these behaviours 'imitative' when the children did not see the model performing them.

WAS THE SAMPLE REPRESENTATIVE?

The sample consisted of 72 children from the same nursery. Although this is a reasonable size, in fact there were only six children in each of the experimental conditions. It is hard to argue that conclusions drawn from just six children can be generalised. The children were all from the same nursery and therefore represent a particular group of children who have all had similar educational/play experiences and therefore may not be representative of all children of that age.

WHAT TYPE OF DATA WAS COLLECTED?

The main data discussed by the authors are quantitative, that is, we are simply given numbers to represent the amount of aggressive/non-aggressive behaviours shown by the children. These data are useful and

CD-ROM

The Developmental Approach: Bandura's experiment

FOR CONSIDERATION

What other information could the researchers have collected?

Are your suggestions quantitative or qualitative?

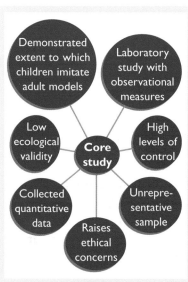

Fig. 3.13 *Evaluating the core study*

allow for some straightforward comparisons to be drawn between the groups. The number of children in each group would make statistical analysis difficult and the quantitative data do not really give a clear picture of the children's actions. Two children may have exhibited the same numbers of aggressive acts but in different ways or to different extents. There are also qualitative data included, such as the comments made by the children, and these are very useful in illustrating the children's experiences and feelings, although they are difficult to analyse statistically.

IS THE STUDY ETHICAL?

The answer to this is 'no'. There is no information given in the study about parental consent and it is highly likely that parents would not have agreed to their children being subjected to this experience. Some of the children were upset and distressed by the aggressive model's behaviour; all of the children were told that some toys were not for them but for some other children; and throughout the experiment the children were on their own with an experimenter whom they did not know very well.

WHAT DOES THE STUDY TELL US …

About the nature-nurture debate?

The study concludes that boys showed more imitative physical aggression than girls and also suggests that children were more upset by the female aggressive model's behaviour. Although it suggests that boys may be more likely to copy aggressive behaviours, we are not able to conclude anything about the nature-nurture debate. It is equally possible that the boys have been reinforced for copying adult male behaviour more than the girls have and that boys may have been reinforced for aggressive behaviour (or girls not reinforced) previously.

About reinforcement?

Although the study considers modelling (or imitation) rather than reinforcement, we can draw some cautious conclusions. There is the suggestion that imitating a same-sex model is more acceptable and this is likely to be because this has been reinforced in the past.

IS THE STUDY USEFUL?

The study has practical applications and is often used by those people who consider that violence on television will be imitated by children. However, the study did not test the effect of televised models, and there may be many differences between the way children understand the behaviour of 'real' people compared to characters on television. The study was useful in demonstrating the extent to which children imitate adult models.

HODGES AND TIZARD (1989): BACKGROUND

WHAT DO CHILDREN NEED?

KEY DEFINITIONS

AFFECTIONLESS PSYCHOPATHY
Lack of emotions; no positive feelings for anyone else and no feelings of guilt.

Fig. 3.14 Rhesus monkey with its surrogate mother (Harlow and Harlow)

 FOR CONSIDERATION

'...The actions of surrogate raised monkeys became bizarre later in life. They engaged in stereotyped behaviour patterns such as clutching themselves and rocking constantly back and forth; they exhibited excessive and misdirected aggression.'

The behaviour of these monkeys as mothers – the motherless mothers as Harlow called them – was very inadequate. These mothers were either indifferent or abusive towards their babies. The indifferent mothers did not nurse, comfort or protect their young, but they did not harm them. The abusive mothers violently bit or otherwise injured their infants, to the point that many of them died.

 FOR CONSIDERATION

Can research with animals tell us anything about human development?

This question has been a central one for psychologists ever since psychology began. **Freud** (see Section 10) has much to say on early mother-child relationships, and the Second World War produced a huge debate about the effects of institutionalisation and **maternal deprivation** on children's later development. Below we look briefly at some of the important theorists in this area.

Bowlby

Bowlby proposed that the mother-child relationship is central to an individual's social and emotional development. Bowlby suggests that difficulties with this relationship can cause emotional and behavioural difficulties in later life. In humans, this relationship is referred to as a **monotropic bond** (monotropy). Bowlby believes that the root of this behaviour is biological, with both offspring and mother's bonding behaviour being genetically determined.

For human offspring, Bowlby states that there is a **critical period** in which the bond must be formed. This period is from birth to approximately 5 years. During this period, any disruption to, or failure of the bond (referred to as **maternal deprivation**), can result in poor social and emotional development, leading to delinquency, depression, learning difficulties, affectionless psychopathy, and so on.

Harlow and Harlow

Research with animals has also added to this debate. Harlow and Harlow (1960) separated new-born Rhesus monkeys from their mothers and reared them (in isolation) with substitute or surrogate mothers made of wire and cloth.

In later life, the monkeys were introduced to their own species. They showed a variety of inappropriate social, sexual and maternal behaviours.

Harlow and Harlow's research supports Bowlby's work on maternal deprivation. The infant monkeys, deprived of their mothers had **abnormal social development**. The neuroscientist Carlson states that the research showed that 'you were not really a monkey unless you were raised in an interactive monkey environment' (1999).

Fig. 3.15 Poor institutional conditions in a Romanian orphanage

WHAT CAN THE RESEARCH TELL US ABOUT CHILDREN IN INSTITUTIONS TODAY?

The issue of children in residential care has been raised many times over recent years. Much research suggests that children brought up in institutions generally fare less well than children in families in terms of social, emotional and intellectual development. Extreme cases of deprivation such as those in the orphanages of Romania after the execution of Ceausescu in 1989 shocked the world. Not only were the children significantly delayed in terms of their physical and motor development but their social development was inappropriate and very similar to the monkeys in Harlow's study. Carlson (1999) describes the Romanian orphans that she studied as 'rocking and grasping themselves', having 'clumsy, sad and inappropriate social interactions', 'superficially friendly but unable to form permanent attachments'.

WHAT IS THE CORE STUDY ABOUT?

The core study by Hodges and Tizard does not consider the effects of extreme deprivation such as those described above. However, it does examine the effects of early institutional care on the social relationships of adolescents. The study is part of a **longitudinal study** that began before the children were 2 years old and reports on their development at age 16. These adolescents had spent the first two years of their lives in institutional care, before being either adopted or restored to their natural families.

The study compared the 'ex-institutional' group with a comparison group of adolescents born and brought up in their biological families and also compared the adolescents who were adopted to the adolescents who were 'restored' to their natural families.

WHO WERE THE PARTICIPANTS?

Thirty-nine ex-institutional children took part: 23 were adopted, 11 were with their biological families (restored) and five were in institutional care. All of the children had spent the first two years of their lives in institutional care.

Comparison groups were set up via approaches to GPs' surgeries and the adolescents were matched on age, sex, one- or two-parent families, occupation of main breadwinner and position in family.

HODGES AND TIZARD (1989): THE CORE STUDY

HOW WAS THE DATA COLLECTED IN THIS STUDY?

There were five different forms of data collection:
- interviews with adolescents
- interviews with mothers (and occasionally fathers)
- self-report questionnaire on social difficulties
- Rutter B scale
- teacher's questionnaire on relationships with peers and teachers.

WHAT WERE THE RESULTS?

Family relationships

Most of the adoptive mothers felt that their child was securely attached to them. This was similar to the comparison group. In contrast, the restored children were described as not securely attached. Adoptive and comparison mothers felt that they loved their child equally (compared to any other children) while this figure was much lower in the restored groups. All of the adoptive mothers thought that the child was as attached or more attached than they had been at age 8, but three of the 'restored' mothers felt that their child was less attached at age 16.

Relationships with siblings

The comparison groups had better relationships with their siblings than the ex-institutional groups, with the restored children experiencing the most problems.

Relationships with siblings

	Results from adolescents' interviews		Results from parents' interviews	
	No difficulties or slight difficulties	Marked difficulties	No difficulties or slight difficulties	Marked difficulties
Ex-institutional adolescents (21)	13	8	12	9
Comparisons (24)	23	1	22	2

Showing affection

At the age of 8, the adopted children had been the most affectionate. At the age of 16, there were no differences between the adopted group and their comparisons, but there were striking differences in the restored group. The restored children were much less affectionate than any of the other groups, with no children in this group described as very affectionate.

Fig. 3.15 What do children need for normal development?

FOR CONSIDERATION

What are the strengths and weaknesses of each of these measures?

REMEMBER

- Parents and especially fathers of restored adolescents had difficulty in showing affection compared to parents of adoptive children who had far less difficulty.
- There were no differences between the ex-institutional group and the comparisons in terms of how similar parents felt the child's views and attitudes were.
- Restored children were described as less involved in family life than adopted children, but there was very little difference between these groups and their comparisons.
- The ex-institutional adolescents were described as having more difficulties with peer relationships than the comparisons. No difference was found between the adopted and restored groups. Ex-institutional children were less likely to have a special friend than the comparison groups and were slightly more likely to be attention seeking. Teachers tended to rate ex-institutional adolescents as 'less popular than their peers' compared to the comparisons (although some were rated as more popular). No differences were found between the adopted and restored children.

Showing affection

	Never or rarely	Routine time only	Very affectionate
Adopted children (22)	9	1	12
Their comparisons (21)	5	2	14
Restored children (10)	7	3	0
Their comparisons (10)	1	2	7

In terms of relations within the family there was very little difference between the adopted group and the comparison group, with both experiencing loving relationships. The restored group however were far less securely attached to their families.

Confiding and support

Mothers in all groups felt that they would know if their child was upset. Over 80 per cent of parents in each group believed that the adolescent would confide in them over at least some anxieties. There was no evidence of differences between ex-institutional and comparison groups.

WHAT ARE THE STUDY'S CONCLUSIONS?

Five key differences between the ex-institutional adolescents and the matched comparisons are suggested:
- the ex-institutional adolescents are more often adult oriented;
- they are more likely to have difficulties in peer relations;
- they are less likely to have a special friend;
- they are less likely to turn to peers for emotional support; and
- they are less likely to be selective in choosing friends.

Hodges and Tizard analysed the data further to see how many of these characteristics were evident in each individual child. They found only two ex-institutional children who showed all five characteristics, but half of this group showed four characteristics. In contrast, only one of the matched comparisons showed four characteristics. The more likely the ex-institutional adolescents were to show these characteristics, the more likely they were to have higher Rutter B scale scores (which measures general emotional and behavioural disturbance). There was some tendency for adolescents with higher scores to be more likely to have been referred to child psychiatric or psychological services but no more likely to have been in trouble with the police.

There is some evidence that early institutional care has an effect on later social relationships. Ex-institutional adolescents differ from matched comparisons in their relationships with peers and adults outside the family. Only the restored group differs from comparisons in terms of relationships within the family.

THINKING LIKE A PSYCHOLOGIST – EVALUATING THE CORE STUDY

WHAT ARE THE STRENGTHS AND WEAKNESSES OF HODGES AND TIZARD'S METHOD?

This study is a longitudinal study, which means that the researchers have collected data from the adolescents at regular intervals since they were very young. Longitudinal studies are valuable sources of data in developmental psychology as they allow change to be monitored. However, they are time consuming as well as expensive and they suffer from **subject attrition**, which is a loss of participants between each data collection. The adolescents may not want to take part any more or may have moved and be untraceable. This can lead to quite large initial samples reducing drastically at later stages of the research.

To counter these problems, some researchers prefer to use **cross-sectional designs** where participants of different ages are tested all at once. This allows the researcher to draw conclusions more quickly but has the problem of subject variability since the researcher is not testing the same people in each age group.

Fig. 3.17 Tools for collecting data

The study also used a variety of **self-report** and **questionnaire/interview methods**. These are valuable tools for collecting data and if they include open-ended questions will allow the researcher to explore issues in detail. However, these methods are subject to several problems, the most important of which is **social desirability.** Can we be sure that participants are telling us the truth when we ask them about this kind of personal information?

WAS THE SAMPLE REPRESENTATIVE?

The sample is quite small by this point in the research and some of the sub-groups such as those restored to their natural parents is very small indeed. It is likely that a much larger sample would be more representative. However, the matching of the ex-institutional children with the comparisons was done on a number of variables and this makes comparisons between the two groups valid ones.

WHAT TYPE OF DATA WAS COLLECTED?

Both **quantitative** and **qualitative** data were collected. Much of the interview material would be qualitative. Qualitative data have the advantage of reflecting the participants' own thoughts and feelings (or at least the thoughts and feelings that they wish you to know) whereas a more quantitative 'forced choice' approach may mean people are being pushed into categories that they would not have put themselves

FOR CONSIDERATION

What other information could have been collected?

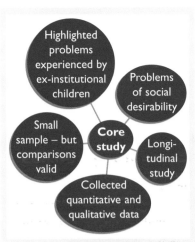

Fig. 3.18 Evaluating the core study

HOT EXAM HINT

You should be able to:
- describe the aim, sample, method, results and conclusion of this study
- discuss the strengths and weaknesses of longitudinal studies and also of the various methods of collecting data.

FOR CONSIDERATION

1 What is subject attrition? Why might a study like this suffer from subject attrition?
2 What differences were found between the ex-institutional adolescents and the comparison groups?
3 What differences were found between the adopted and restored groups? How might these differences be explained?
4 What other areas of developmental psychology might be investigated using longitudinal studies?

into. However, if a study like this collected only qualitative data, it would be almost impossible to draw any general conclusions from the research due to the problems associated with coding the material that had been collected. Asking people to respond using predetermined categories may not be ideal, but it does allow easy statistical analysis of the data, which means comparisons can be made.

WHAT DOES THE STUDY TELL US ABOUT THE NATURE-NURTURE DEBATE?

The study strongly indicates a **negative effect** of early institutionalisation, although it also suggests that many of these effects can be overcome. These findings strongly support the 'nurture' side of the nature-nurture debate as it is clear that the social relationships of all the adolescents questioned in the study were the result of the type of experiences they had had during their lives.

IS THE STUDY USEFUL?

The study is very useful in highlighting the problems experienced by ex-institutional children. These results could be applied to suggest how children in care should be looked after. For example, the importance of an **attachment figure** would appear to be crucial for social development. If children are cared for by many temporary carers, this is likely to have a harmful effect on their long-term development. The study also suggests that adoption is highly successful and this again could have useful implications for those who are involved in making decisions about children in care.

Fig. 3.19 Sigmund Freud

WHAT DID FREUD CONTRIBUTE TO PSYCHOLOGY?

Freud wrote many books and it is impossible to do justice to his ideas here. He was one of the first theorists to propose that the *mind could affect the body*, that is, that physical disorders could have psychological causes. This is a widely accepted view now but was highly controversial at the time, especially as Freud proposed that infants had sexual feelings, a view that shocked the Victorian establishment. We now know that Freud had originally proposed that many of the female patients he was treating had been sexually abused by their parents but changed his theories to suggest that these experiences were 'fantasies', possibly due to the reception his views received. It was to be many years before society accepted that these original claims might be true.

Freud's theory proposes that sexuality in childhood consists of the wish to 'possess' the parent of the opposite sex, not the act itself. He claimed that this wish is present in all children, whether or not they develop 'hysterical disorders' in later life.

WHAT IS INFANTILE SEXUALITY?

Freud proposed that much of our personality is unconscious, but that this unconscious mind determines much of our behaviour.

Freud used hypnosis, analysis of dreams and free association to collect evidence about his patients' unconscious memories and desires and interpreted this evidence to understand how their personalities had been shaped. An important concept in understanding the development of personality is **libido.** Libido is not simply sexual energy in Freudian theory but is life energy and is behind a whole range of activities from affection between parents and children to sexual relationships between adults.

Freud suggested that children pass through several stages of **psycho-sexual development** in which the libido is focused upon different parts of the body. The first stage is the **oral stage** (the first two years of life) and, in this stage, the libido is focused on the mouth. Infants experience pleasure from sucking and biting. Early in this stage, the child has no understanding of the boundaries between themselves and other people and does not recognise that the mother is a separate person. In a sense, then, the infant does not recognise that someone else is responsible for satisfying their needs. The infant cannot love the mother as they have not yet learned to distinguish her from themselves and loves only the breast as a source of food and oral pleasure.

- When Freud describes children's behaviour as sexual he simply means that this behaviour has the same origin as sexual behaviour.
- If the child's needs are not satisfied in the oral stage, Freud suggested that fixation might occur and this would result in adults who are incapable of personal love for others. Rather they will treat people as objects and spend their adult lives seeking oral satisfaction.
- Fixation can occur at the anal stage, too. Harsh toilet training can lead to obsessive or compulsive behaviours.

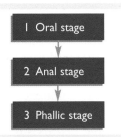

Fig. 3.20 *Stages of psycho-sexual development (Freud)*

KEY CONCEPTS

- Oedipus is the hero of a Greek tragedy in which he kills his father and marries his mother. Freud suggests that this is every young boy's fantasy. He describes a similar complex for girls called the Electra complex, but the core study we are considering deals only with the Oedipus complex.
- When the little boy identifies with the father, he develops a **superego**, the part of the personality that contains moral and social standards. They have internalised the same-sex parent.

The second stage is the **anal stage** and the libido shifts to the anus. Children gain pleasure from achieving control over their own bodies and this will include retaining and eliminating faeces as well as developing other physical skills. In many cultures, this is when toilet training happens and this can be a source of pleasure or distress to the child depending on how this is handled by the parents.

Around the age of 3 or 4, the libido becomes focused on the genitals and children begin to display an interest in the differences between boys and girls as well developing a strong attachment to the parent of the opposite sex. Freud calls this the **phallic stage** and the attachment to the mother by the son is referred to as the **Oedipus complex.**

What is the Oedipus complex?

Very simply, the young boy begins to wish for exclusive relationship with his mother. He is jealous of his father as his mother has a relationship with his father that seems to exclude him. He may be afraid that his father will punish him for his feelings towards his mother and if the father shows irritation at the son's attachment to his mother or his growing fascination with sexual organs, this fear will be intensified. Freud suggested that the boy suffers from **castration anxiety** – the ultimate punishment from the father.

How can the young boy resolve the Oedipus complex?

Little boys are in a frightening situation. Their mothers appear to reject their advances and they may feel that they prefer the father. They believe that their fathers are angry with them and so to resolve this, they must become as much like their fathers as possible. This will ensure that their fathers are not angry with them as well as appearing to be like their fathers in their mother's eyes.

WHAT IS THE CORE STUDY ABOUT?

This study is a case study of a child, which Freud offers as evidence for the existence of the Oedipus complex.

FREUD (1909): THE CORE STUDY

WHAT WAS THE AIM OF THE STUDY?

The study was used to illustrate Freud's theory of the Oedipus complex (part of the phallic stage of Freud's theory of psycho-sexual development).

WHAT WAS THE METHOD?

This is a **case study,** involving only one participant.

WHO IS THE CASE STUDY ABOUT?

The study concerns a young boy called **Hans.** Hans was born in 1903 and his family were great admirers of Freud's work. His father was a doctor who wrote lengthy reports about Hans' behaviour and then sent them to Freud for comments. As Hans' parents were admirers of Freud, they were bringing Hans up in a relatively liberal way for the time in the hope that he would not develop any of the adult neuroses that Freud described in his adult patients. Hans' father had been communicating with Freud since Hans was 3 years old, but when Hans was 5, the doctor wrote to Freud describing the development of a phobia (fear) of horses.

Fig. 3.21 Hans and his father

HOW DID FREUD INTERPRET HANS' PHOBIA?

Freud suggested that Hans' fear of horses was symbolic of his fear of his father and therefore evidence for the Oedipus complex. Hans was particularly afraid of white horses with black around the mouth and wearing blinkers and Freud suggests that this resembled Hans' father as he had white skin, a moustache and wore glasses. Further, he also quotes Hans as saying 'Daddy, don't trot away from me' and 'Daddy, you are so white'. Hans and his father are described as playing horses regularly in a game where Hans' father would pretend to be a horse so that Hans could ride on his back. Finally, the fact that Hans was afraid that the horse would bite him was interpreted by Freud as symbolising the fear that his father would castrate him.

WHAT OTHER EVIDENCE IS DESCRIBED?

Freud describes several other pieces of evidence in support of his theory of psycho-sexual development. There are many references to Hans' fascination with his penis (which he called his 'widdler') and his desire to find out which people (and objects) had one and which did not. Freud actually states that when Hans was 3 years old his mother had found him with his hand on his penis and threatened to 'send for Doctor A to cut off your widdler'. This evidence is used as

Extract from Hans' conversation with his father:

Hans: It's only in the big bath that I'm afraid of falling in.
Father: But mummy baths you in it. Are you afraid of mummy dropping you in the water?
Hans: I'm afraid of her letting go and my head going in.
Father: But you know Mummy's fond of you and won't let go of you.
Hans: I only just thought it.
Father: Why?
Hans: I don't know.
Father: Perhaps it was because you'd been naughty and thought she didn't love you any more?
Hans: Yes.
Father: When you were watching mummy giving Hanna her bath, perhaps you wished she would let go of her so Hanna should fall in?
Hans: Yes.

Freud interprets this as Han's hostility towards his sister who he sees as usurping his place in his mother's affections and that he is unconsciously treating his father and sister in the same way as they have both taken his mother away from him.

support for the proposal that Hans is in the phallic stage of development.

Hans' mother had a baby girl when Hans was three years old. This event is discussed at length by Freud and he describes an incident reported to him by Hans' father. Hans had developed a fear of the bath and his father questioned him about it (see opposite).

Freud also gives us information about Hans' dreams, which was communicated to him by Hans' father. Hans dreamt about two giraffes, a big one and a crumpled one. 'The big one called out because I took the crumpled one away from it. Then it stopped calling out and then I sat down on top of the crumpled one.'

Freud interprets this dream as symbolic of Hans' Oedipal wish to take his mother away from his father. In another dream, Hans reported that he had been grown up with his own children. Their mother was Hans' mother and Hans' father was their grandfather. This dream is more obviously a fantasy of being married to his own mother and it is interesting that Hans' unconscious mind has resolved the issue of his father by making him the grandfather.

WHAT ARE THE STUDY'S CONCLUSIONS?

This is only some of the evidence described by Freud. The original case study is reported in a book and is well over 100 pages long. At the end of the case study, Freud concludes that Hans was experiencing the Oedipus complex and has used this case to support his notions of infantile sexuality, his theories of psycho-sexual development and his writings generally on phobias.

THINKING LIKE A PSYCHOLOGIST – EVALUATING THE CORE STUDY

WHAT ARE THE STRENGTHS AND WEAKNESSES OF FREUD'S METHOD?

Case studies have both strengths and weaknesses. They allow for detailed examinations of individuals and are often conducted in clinical settings so that the results are applied to helping that particular individual, as is the case here. However, Freud also tries to use this case to support his theories of child development generally. Case studies should not be used to make generalisations about larger groups of people.

There are several other weaknesses with the way that the data were collected. Freud only met Hans once and all of his information came from the boy's father. We have already seen that Hans' father was an admirer of Freud's theories and tried to put them into practice with his son. This means that he would have been biased in the way he interpreted and reported Hans' behaviour to Freud. There are also examples of leading questions in the way that Hans' father questioned Hans about his feelings (see the extract on page 65 for an example of this).

Finally, there are problems with the conclusions that Freud reaches. He claims that Hans recovered fully from his phobia when his father sat him down and reassured him that he was not going to castrate him and one can only wonder about the effects of this conversation on a small child!

More importantly, is Freud right in his conclusions that Hans' phobia was the result of the Oedipus complex or might there be a more straightforward explanation? Hans had seen a horse fall down in the street and thought it was dead. This happened very soon after Hans had attended a funeral and was beginning to question his parents about death. A behaviourist explanation would be simply that Hans was frightened by the horse falling over and developed a phobia as a result of this experience. Slap (an American psychoanalyst) argues that Hans' phobia may have another explanation. Shortly after the beginning of the phobia (after Hans had seen the horse fall down), Hans had to have his tonsils out. After this, the phobia worsened and it was then that he specifically identified white horses as the ones he was afraid of. Slap suggests that the masked and gowned surgeon (all in white) may have significantly contributed to Hans' fears.

CD-ROM

The developmental approach: Freud's psychosexual stages, Freudian dreams and Web investigation: Freud

Fig. 3.22 Hans' fears

HOT EXAM HINT

You should be able to:
- describe the way in which Freud collected the data in this case study and the conclusions he drew from the data
- discuss problems with the data collecting methods and offer alternative explanations of the data
- describe the strengths and weaknesses of case studies.

FOR CONSIDERATION

Give examples of leading questions from the study.

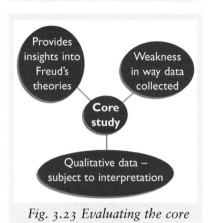

Fig. 3.23 Evaluating the core study

FOR CONSIDERATION

1 What is the Oedipus complex? What evidence does Freud offer that suggests that Hans was in the Oedipus complex?
2 What criticisms could be made of Freud's methods of collecting data in this case study?
3 How did Freud explain Hans' phobia of horses? How else might this phobia be explained?
4 What are the strengths and weaknesses of case studies?

WHAT TYPE OF DATA WAS COLLECTED?

The data are all **qualitative** and have been subject to interpretation, first by Hans' father and then by Freud. The reports of Hans' conversations with his father are fascinating, especially when you remember that Hans was only 4 or 5 years old during most of this time. The leading questions would suggest than Hans' father 'put words in his mouth' on several occasions.

ARE THERE ANY ETHICAL ISSUES?

Apart from the issues of leading questions and the reliability of child evidence, you could consider whether any potential harm may have been done to Hans as a result of this study. It could be argued that some of the questions asked by Hans' father may have upset or embarassed the child, or may have made him worry about a variety of issues. Reassuringly, Freud reports that he met Hans as a young man and described him as perfectly normal!

IS THE STUDY USEFUL?

This is a difficult question to answer. It offers us a fascinating insight into Freud's theories and raises a number of questions about the origins of phobias. Freud's work is still highly influential despite some major revisions to his ideas. **The idea of the unconscious mind affecting the physical health of a person and the need for interpretation of material by a therapist are now widely accepted.**

Freud only met Hans once

Leading questions

questions upset Hans.

generalise from case study

Problems with Freuds methods

reliability

Leading questions

biased father.

USEFUL RESOURCES

HOT EXAM HINTS

STRENGTHS OF THE DEVELOPMENTAL APPROACH INCLUDE:

- We can see the effects of maturation (aging) on behaviour (e.g. Samuel and Bryant).
- We can see the effects of experience on behaviour (Bandura).
- Longitudinal research is a valuable way of investigating change (Hodges and Tizard).

WEAKNESSES OF THE DEVELOPMENTAL APPROACH ARE:

- Some research is unethical.
- Longitudinal studies suffer from subject attrition.
- Case studies are difficult to generalize from.
- Laboratory studies may have low ecological validity.

CD-ROM

Revision: Crosswords: Developmental

BOOKS

Gross, R. (2001) *Psychology: The Science of Mind of Behaviour.* Hodder & Stoughton, 4th edn.
This is an excellent general psychology textbook and chapters 29, 32, 34 and 35 will give you plenty of information on the topics covered in this section.

Donaldson, M. (1984) *Children's Minds*, Flamingo.
This is a classic text considering the impact of Piaget's work and the variety of research that it generated. This easy-to-read text covers the criticisms that have been made of Piaget's methods and summarises many interesting studies. Look for the naughty teddy study by McGarrigle!

Donaldson, M. (1992) *Human Minds: An Exploration*, Penguin.
A more wide ranging book than the one described above, this looks at emotional development throughout life.

There are lots of easy-to-read books on Freud. Try this one:
Berry, R. (2000) *Freud: A Beginner's Guide*, Hodder & Stoughton.

If you are interested in the criticisms made of Freud's theory, then the following books are fascinating reading:
Masson, J. (1992) *Final Analysis. The Making and Unmaking of a Psychoanalyst,* Fontana.
Masson, J. (1992) *The Assault on Truth. Freud and Child Sexual Abuse,* Fontana.

WEBSITES

Go to www.heinemann.co.uk/hotlinks and insert the code 670XP.
Look at the websites listed under Developmental: Useful websites.

CHAPTER 4

THE PHYSIOLOGICAL APPROACH

THE CORE STUDIES

WHAT IS PHYSIOLOGICAL PSYCHOLOGY?

Physiological psychology (sometimes called bio-psychology) considers the extent to which behaviour and experience is determined by our biology. In particular, physiological psychologists have concentrated on studying the structure and functions of the brain and the nervous system.

THE CORE STUDIES

Schachter and Singer (1962)

This is a **laboratory experiment** which aimed to establish whether emotions are purely physiological responses to external events or whether there is a role for cognitive processes. The study concludes that cognitive appraisal of a situation is a crucial element in the experience of an emotion.

Dement and Kleitman (1957)

This is another laboratory study which looked at the relationship between rapid eye movements (REM) when asleep and dreaming. Although this link is fairly well known now, Dement and Kleitman were the first researchers to establish this objectively.

Sperry (1968)

This is a **quasi-experiment** which studied a number of individuals who had had the two hemispheres of their brain separated as a cure for extreme epilepsy. Sperry developed groundbreaking techniques that revealed fascinating information about the functioning of the two hemispheres of the brain.

Raine, Buchsbaum and LaCasse (1997)

This is another quasi-experiment which used state-of-the-art technology (PET scans) to investigate brain activity in people who had committed murder but claimed that they were not guilty by reason of insanity. Raine *et al.*'s results demonstrated significant differences between the brain activity of these people and a control group in areas of the brain that are known to control aggressive and emotional behaviours.

SCHACHTER AND SINGER (1962): BACKGROUND

WHAT ARE EMOTIONS?

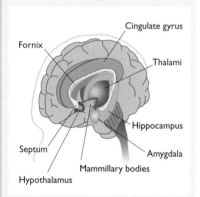

Fig. 4.1 The limbic system

We all know what emotions are, but putting this into words has proved extremely difficult. As Green (1994) has noted, 'Psychology has had a great deal of trouble even defining emotion, let alone analysing and identifying the underlying mechanisms'. Green goes on to attempt a description of the characteristics of emotions and his description demonstrates the importance of both **physiological arousal** and **cognitive processing** in emotional experience. The relative roles of these two factors are considered by the core study conducted by Schachter and Singer.

While some emotions may be universal (that is, displayed by most living things) such as disgust, fear, anger and parental love, other emotions are more complex. Carter (1998) describes emotions as:

'sophisticated cognitive constructs that are arrived at only after considerable processing by the conscious mind and an elaborate exchange of information between the conscious cortical areas of the brain and the limbic system beneath'.

Carter gives the example of 'the pleasure-tinged-with-guilt' that might be felt when someone sends you a birthday card and you realise that you forgot to send them one. She explains that the card itself does not produce this emotional response. This arises only after **cognitive processing of the memories and associations** produced by the experience of receiving the card. This is important as it highlights the role of cognitive processes in emotional experience.

HOW HAVE EMOTIONS BEEN INVESTIGATED?

There has been a great deal of research into brain mechanisms of emotion, usually in non-human animals. This research has highlighted the role of certain brain areas in emotional responses, for example the **limbic system** controls emotion responses. Damage to the **amygdala** can produce changes in aggressive behaviour.

THE ROLES OF AROUSAL AND COGNITION

The James-Lange theory

This theory proposed that external stimuli cause specific physiological responses (such as adrenalin release and increased heart rate) and that this is 'felt' as emotion. In this theory, the physiological response is both necessary and sufficient for the occurrence of an emotional state. In other words, there is no need for cognitive processing for an emotion to be 'felt'.

A Portugese psychologist, Moniz, was so impressed with the calming effects of lesions to the frontal lobes in monkeys that he applied this research to humans. Moniz performed the first 'frontal lobotomies' on human patients and it is estimated that some 50,000 lobotomies were performed in the 1940s and 1950s. Although the psychologists performing these operations claimed their success, it is clear that many 'lobotomised' patients were left in an almost vegetative state.

 FOR CONSIDERATION

CRITICISMS OF THE JAMES-LANGE THEORY

This theory can be criticised as it assumes that all emotions have different patterns of physiological arousal and this has not been supported by research. Further, the physiological changes do not occur as quickly as we feel emotions and it is possible to experience physiological arousal without experiencing emotion (such as after taking exercise).

 FOR CONSIDERATION

CRITICISMS OF THE CANNON-BARD THEORY

The Cannon-Bard theory can be criticised for assuming that physiological changes have no influence on emotion. There are several studies that indicate that these do have a role. The theory also overestimated the role of the thalamus – there are several studies indicating important roles for other brain areas. Furthermore, much of the evidence presented for this theory is based on animal research.

The Cannon-Bard theory

The Cannon-Bard theory proposes that emotion eliciting external stimuli produces two separate reactions: first, the thalamus sends signals to the hypothalamus to trigger the physiological responses; second, the thalamus sends signals to the cortex which are registered as fear. In this theory, the physiological response is neither necessary nor sufficient for the occurrence of emotion.

HOW HAVE THE THEORIES BEEN TESTED?

The first major study of the role of arousal and cognition was conducted by Maranon in 1924. He injected his subjects with adrenalin to produce a state of physiological arousal. If the James-Lange theory was correct, subjects should experience emotion as a direct result of this physiological arousal. This was not what Maranon found as over two-thirds of his subjects reported just the physiological effects of the adrenalin (increased heart rate, dry mouth) and the rest described the experience 'as if' they were feeling an emotion but did not feel the emotion. The conclusion drawn by Maranon was that physiological arousal alone was not enough for the experience of emotion.

The next major study of emotion was the core study conducted by Schachter and Singer. They manipulated arousal by giving injections of adrenalin but then proposed that subjects would interpret this arousal in terms of the 'available cognitions', that is, the environmental cues that are available to them.

They claim that this is what they found and this led to the **Cognitive Labelling theory** (or TWO-FACTOR theory) which proposes that external stimuli cause general physiological responses and that these must be interpreted (cognitive appraisal) as a particular emotional feeling. In this theory, physiological arousal is necessary but is not sufficient for the experience of emotion as cognitive appraisal may label the same physiological arousal in a number of different ways. We consider their research and the validity of their conclusions in the next two sections.

SCHACHTER AND SINGER (1962): THE CORE STUDY

The participants were 184 male college students studying psychology at the University of Minnesota. They received two extra points in their exam for every hour they served as experimental participants.

Information given to participants

Condition	Information
Epinephrine – informed	Told correct effects (heart rate, respiration rate, etc.)
Epinephrine – ignorant	Told nothing
Epinephrine – misinformed	Told incorrect effects (numb feet, itching, headache)
Placebo (control)	Told nothing

 ## KEY DEFINITIONS

PLACEBO
An inactive or fake substance that is given 'as if' it were the real substance. Placebo effects can be very strong.

KEY CONCEPT

Epinephrine produces increases in blood pressure, heart rate and respiration rate.

WHAT WAS THE AIM OF THE STUDY?

Schachter and Singer proposed that if you experience a state of physiological arousal for which you have no immediate explanation, you will interpret this state in terms of the **cognitions** available to you (that is, the situation you are in). If an adequate explanation has been provided, you will not need to do this.

HOW WAS EMOTION MANIPULATED?

The first variable – the state of **physiological arousal** – was manipulated by deceiving participants into thinking that they were participating in a study on the effects of vitamin injections on vision. Participants consented to be given an injection of suproxin, but they either received an injection of adrenalin (epinephrine) or a **placebo**.

The second variable (**available explanation**) was manipulated by the information given to the participants – see the table in the margin.

Finally, the **emotional environment** was also manipulated. Participants were allocated to either the **euphoria** condition or the **anger** condition.

Immediately after the injection, the participant was put into a room with a confederate (or stooge).

In the euphoria condition, the stooge doodled on paper, crumpled it up and tossed it round the room, made paper aeroplanes, built a tower out of paper folders, knocked it down and played with a hula hoop.

In the anger condition, the participant and the stooge were given questionnaires to fill in. These questions began fairly innocently (for example, 'List all the foods you have had to eat today') but became increasingly personal and included 'Do you ever hear bells?', ' What is your father's annual income?' and finally, ' How many times each week do you have sexual intercourse?'. The stooge became increasingly annoyed by these questions, making comments such as 'It's none of their business, I'm leaving this one blank' and finally, 'The hell with it, I don't have to tell them all this'. He ripped up the questionnaire and stormed out of the room.

HOW WAS EMOTION MEASURED?

- **Standardised observation** of behaviour through a one-way mirror. For example, in the euphoria condition did the participant join in, initiate new games, or ignore the stooge?

It was important that the stooge's routine began very quickly after the injection so that participants did not have time to feel the effects of the injection and begin to interpret it.

The seven conditions

Euphoria condition	Anger condition
Epinephrine – informed	Epinephrine – informed
Epinephrine – ignorant	Epinephrine – ignorant
Epinephrine – misinformed	
Placebo	Placebo

The epinephrine-misinformed group was not subjected to the anger condition. Schachter and Singer explain that this was the control condition: its inclusion in the euphoria condition alone would be enough to draw conclusions about the effect of misinforming participants. This left seven conditions to examine, as shown here.

Fig. 4.2 Would you join in?

- **Self-reports** of emotional states. Participants were asked to complete a questionnaire containing a number of filler questions about hunger, fatigue, etc., as well as some 'critical' questions including:
  – 'How irritated, angry or annoyed would you say you feel at present?' (rated from 0–4)
  – 'How good or happy would you say you feel at the present?' (rated from 0–4)

WHAT WERE THE RESULTS?

A score for emotional state was calculated by subtracting the self-report score for irritation from the self-report score for happiness. The higher the positive value, the happier the participant reports himself as feeling.

The results

Euphoria condition	Self-report score	Anger condition	Self-report score
Epinephrine – informed	0.98	Epinephrine – informed	1.91
Epinephrine – ignorant	1.78	Epinephrine – ignorant	1.39
Epinephrine – misinformed	1.90		
Placebo (control)	1.61	Placebo (control)	1.63

WHAT ARE THE STUDY'S CONCLUSIONS?

In the epinephrine ignorant and epinephrine misinformed conditions the participants do not have an **appropriate explanation** of their physiological state. They are more likely to use the **situational cognitions** to label their feelings.

The behavioural reports support this conclusion. Participants in the euphoria epinephrine ignorant and euphoria epinephrine misinformed joined in with significantly more of the stooges' activities than the participants in the euphoria epinephrine informed or euphoria placebo conditions. In the anger conditions the participants did not go along with the complaints as much as had been expected, but there is still a highly significant difference between the observed behaviour of the informed and ignorant groups. The anger epinephrine ignorant group showed more angry behaviour, suggesting that the informed participants had a satisfactory explanation of their bodily states and did not need to refer to the cognitions provided by the stooges' angry behaviour. The fact that the epinephrine ignorant participants were also significantly more angry than the placebo participants suggests that the epinephrine appears to have led participants to an angrier state than those who received the placebo injections.

The hypothesis is *confirmed*. If participants had no explanation for their state of arousal, they used the available situation cues. This did not happen where a satisfactory explanation had been provided.

THINKING LIKE A PSYCHOLOGIST – EVALUATING THE CORE STUDY

WHAT ARE THE STRENGTHS AND WEAKNESSES OF SCHACHTER AND SINGER'S METHOD?

The method used in this study was a laboratory experiment which allows for a high level of control over variables as well as **random allocation to conditions**. However, laboratory studies often lack ecological validity.

WAS THE SAMPLE REPRESENTATIVE?

FOR CONSIDERATION

What if this study had been conducted with a different sample? Do you think the results might have been different?

The sample used in the study consisted of 184 undergraduate students who received course credits for participating in the research. Firstly, undergraduate students may not be representative of the general population and secondly, the offer of course credits may increase the likelihood that the students behaved in ways that they thought the experimenters wanted them to behave (demand characteristics).

WHAT TYPE OF DATA WAS COLLECTED?

The data collected were quantitative, although there were two different methods of data collection. The first measure of emotion was taken from self-reports where participants had to rate their feelings on a 0–4 scale. Self-reports of this type have several weaknesses. First, different participants may interpret the scale in different ways and this may mean that participants with very similar levels of emotion actually rate themselves very differently. Second, participants may not tell the truth when asked questions like these. This may be due to demand characteristics or to **social desirability bias**.

Fig. 4.3 Observers watched through a one-way mirror

The second measure of emotion was **behavioural observation**. Observers watched the participants through one-way mirrors and recorded their behaviours using a number of predetermined categories. Observation can be a useful method of data collection especially if people do not realise that they are being observed (although this may raise ethical issues), but the categories need to be carefully defined and the observers trained in order to ensure that observations are reliable.

It could be argued that collecting the two different measures of emotion in this study is a strength as they provide some kind of comparison. If the self-reports and the behavioural observations agree, then this increases the reliability of the conclusions.

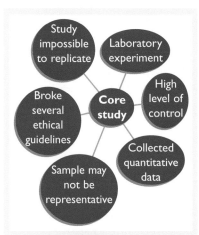

Fig. 4.4 Evaluating the core study

IS THE STUDY ETHICAL?

The study broke several ethical guidelines. The main ethical concern is the issue of deception. Participants were deceived in several ways: they were told that the injection was a vitamin when it was epinephrine; they were misled (to various degrees) about the effects that the injection would have on them; they were led to believe that the 'stooge' was another participant; and they were not aware that their behaviour was being observed through one-way mirrors. The study could also have caused distress to the participants, particularly those in the anger conditions, who may have been very offended by the questions that they were asked.

DOES THE STUDY GIVE AN INDIVIDUAL OR A SITUATIONAL EXPLANATION OF BEHAVIOUR?

The authors conclude that our emotional experiences are a result of cognitive appraisal of the situation we find ourselves in. In this sense, they are offering a situational explanation for behaviour (emotions) although as we will see below, this conclusion may have been slightly overstated.

IS THE STUDY USEFUL?

It could be argued that the conclusions drawn from the study helped to resolve the debate between the James-Lange and the Cannon-Bard theories of emotion. Schachter and Singer conclude that there are not specific patterns of arousal associated with each emotion but a general pattern of arousal which is combined with cognitive appraisal to determine the emotion. Therefore, physiological arousal is necessary, but not sufficient. However, there are problems with this conclusion.

First, it has proved impossible to replicate this study (and today it would be considered too unethical to replicate). Second, the conclusions may be overstated. It is possible that participants are simply more suggestible when under the influence of adrenalin and therefore imitate the stooge more. This would go some way to explaining why the self-reports and the observer ratings are different (see above). Finally, the initial analysis of the data revealed only one difference (between the observer ratings of emotion between epinephrine ignorant and placebo groups in the anger condition). It was only when the researchers excluded participants who they decided had worked out the aim of the study that they found differences in the observer ratings for the euphoria conditions. All of these criticisms would suggest that Schachter and Singer may have overstated their conclusions.

DEMENT AND KLEITMAN (1957): BACKGROUND

WHAT IS SLEEP?

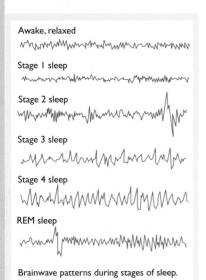

Brainwave patterns during stages of sleep.

Fig. 4.5 Stages of sleep

Sleep consists of a number of stages which are shown by distinctive EEG patterns (see Fig. 4.5):

• Stage 1 sleep is characterised by lowered heart rate, muscle tension and body temperature and is very similar to states of deep relaxation and hypnosis. An EEG recording of brain activity would show alpha waves which have a frequency of 8–12 cycles per second (Hertz). People can be woken easily from this stage of sleep.

• Stage 2 sleep is characterised by slower and larger EEG waves and by the presence of sleep spindles which are bursts of high frequency waves (12–16 Hertz) lasting for about one second. This is a deeper sleep than Stage 1 but people can still be woken fairly easily.

• In Stage 3 sleep delta waves are seen. These are large slow waves of around 1–3 Hertz. People in Stage 3 sleep do not easily respond to external stimuli and are quite difficult to wake up.

• Stage 4 sleep is characterised by delta waves of about 1 Hertz and is the deepest of the four stages of sleep. Metabolic activity is very low and people are difficult to wake, although noises which are personally significant such as a baby crying will waken parents quite easily.

It takes about 30 minutes to reach Stage 4 sleep and we spend a further 30 minutes in this stage before the cycle of sleep reverses through Stages 3 and 2. Instead of entering Stage 1 sleep again, we enter a phase of 'active sleep'. This is where an EEG shows the desynchronised pattern of an aroused subject. Metabolic activity increases, as does heart rate, although the body is more or less paralysed. This is the hardest stage to wake someone from. It is also the deepest stage of sleep and is called **rapid eye movement (REM) sleep** as rapid eye movements can be observed under the closed eyelids. It is sometimes called **paradoxical sleep** because the person is deeply asleep but the brain shows an EEG pattern similar to that of being awake. People typically spend 10 or 15 minutes in REM sleep and then descend through the stages to Stage 4 sleep. This cycle take around 70–90 minutes and is repeated five or six times during a night's sleep.

KEY CONCEPT

Did you know that porpoises sleep with one half of their brain at a time? This is thought to be an evolutionary mechanism that means they can always be aware of predators.

WHY DO WE SLEEP?

- **Restoration theory** suggests that non REM sleep restores bodily processes that have deteriorated during the day and that REM sleep stimulates protein synthesis which replenishes brain processes.
- **Evolutionary theory** suggests that sleep serves a survival function by keeping animals safe from predators. Hibernation would be seen as an extension of this process.

WHY DO WE DREAM?

Some more recent theories have concluded that we sleep because we have a psychological need to dream. Theories of dreaming include the following:

- **Re-organisation of mental structures.** It has been suggested that REM sleep is involved in the organisation of schemas (the cognitive structures which make up our knowledge and understanding) and this is supported by the finding that complex cognitive tasks lead to an increase in the time spent in REM sleep and also by the fact that babies spend so much time in REM sleep.

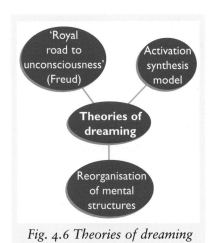

Fig. 4.6 Theories of dreaming

- **The activation synthesis model** proposes that dreams are an 'active interpretation' of the signals produced by the cortex during REM sleep. Crick and Mitchinson (1983) suggest that this is a way of sorting out all the information that has been taken in during the day and so dreaming is about the brain deciding what to keep and what to forget. This could be understood as being similar to a computer system needing to de-bug itself.

- Freud saw dreams as the **'royal road to the unconscious'** and psychoanalytic therapists still use dream interpretation as a way of interpreting the hidden desires and thoughts of the patient.

FOR CONSIDERATION

Look up Freud's theory on dreams. Do you agree with his proposal that the interpretation of dreams can reveal the contents of the unconscious mind?

The core study by Dement and Kleitman described in the next section is a very early laboratory study which established a link between REM sleep and dreaming.

DEMENT AND KLEITMAN (1957): THE CORE STUDY

WHAT WAS THE AIM OF THE STUDY?

The study was an attempt to work out the relationship between eye movements and dreaming. It asked three questions:
- Will people be more likely to report dreams if they are woken during periods of rapid eye movement (REM) than during periods of no REM (NREM)?
- Can people accurately estimate the time spent dreaming?
- Is the direction of eye movement during REM related to dream content?

WHO WERE THE PARTICIPANTS?

They included seven adult males and two adult females. Five of the participants were studied intensively and little data were gathered from the other four.

HOW WAS THE RESEARCH CARRIED OUT?

The study was a laboratory experiment. The participant reported to the sleep laboratory just before their normal bedtime. They had been asked to avoid caffeine and alcohol on the day of the experiment but otherwise to eat normally.

Electrodes were attached near the eyes to measure the eye movement and to the scalp to measure brainwave activity (to find out depth of sleep). The participant then went to bed in a quiet, dark room in the laboratory.

At various times during the night the participant was woken up to test their dream recall. They were woken by a doorbell and spoke into a tape recorder near the bed. They had to state first whether they had been dreaming and if they had, to report the content of the dream.

WHAT WERE THE RESULTS?

Question 1

Question 1 results

Woken during REM sleep		Woken during NREM sleep	
Recalled dreams	**No recall**	**Recalled dreams**	**No recall**
152	39	11	9

The results show that participants were much more likely to recall dreams in REM sleep than in NREM sleep.

Fig. 4.7 William Dement

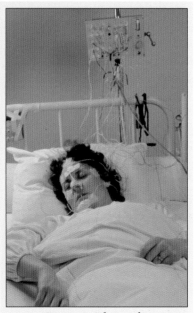

Fig. 4.8 Electrodes were attached to measure participants' eye movements and brainwave activity

Question 2

Participants were woken randomly, either 5 or 15 minutes into REM sleep, and were asked to decide whether they had been dreaming for 5 or 15 minutes.

Question 2 results

Woken after 5 minutes of REM		Woken after 15 minutes of REM	
Correct	**Incorrect**	**Correct**	**Incorrect**
45	6	47	13

The results show that participants were accurate in the estimation of dream length. Interestingly, one participant was responsible for a large number of the incorrect estimates.

CD-ROM

The Physiological Approach: Web investigation: Dement and Kleitman

Question 3

Participants were awoken when one of four main patterns of eye movements had lasted for at least one minute and were asked to describe whet they had been dreaming about. These four patterns and the types of dreams reported are shown in the table.

Question 3 results

Type of eye movement	Number	Examples of dream content
Mainly vertical	3	Standing at the bottom of a cliff and looking up at climbers Climbing ladders and looking up and down Throwing basketballs at a net
Mainly horizontal	I	Watching two people throw tomatoes at each other
Both vertical and horizontal	21	Looking at close objects Talking to groups of people Looking for something Fighting with someone
Very little or none	10	Watching things in the distance Staring at an object Driving a car and staring at the road ahead

KEY CONCEPT

This was a very important finding at the time, as this link had not been shown experimentally before Dement and Kleitman's research.

These results support the idea that eye movement is related to dream content and this is further confirmed by measuring the eye movements of awake subjects looking at close and distant objects.

WHAT WERE THE CONCLUSIONS?

The researchers concluded that there is a correlation between REM sleep and dreaming.

THINKING LIKE A PSYCHOLOGIST – EVALUATING THE CORE STUDY

WHAT ARE THE STRENGTHS AND WEAKNESSES OF DEMENT AND KLEITMAN'S METHOD?

The study was a laboratory experiment. Laboratory studies have high levels of control over variables but may lack ecological validity (see below). The study used the electroencephalograph (EEG) to measure brain activity and this allows precise measurements to be taken.

WAS THE SAMPLE REPRESENTATIVE?

Nine participants were studied in total and only five of these were studied intensively. This is a very small number of participants to generalise from. It could be argued that physiological processes are likely to be the same in all people, but this may not be the case. It is possible that sleep patterns and, in particular, relationships between eye movements and dreaming vary from person to person and the conclusions drawn from Dement and Kleitman's research would be strengthened if the same relationships were established in a larger sample of people.

WHAT TYPE OF DATA WAS COLLECTED?

The data collected were mostly quantitative. For the first two research questions, the data were simply numbers of participants who could/could not recall dreams or who could/could not accurately estimate the length of their dreams. Quantitative data are relatively easy to collect and can be analysed statistically. However, they reduce complex qualitative phenomena to numbers and this often results in a lack of detail in the data. The data collected for the third question were more qualitative as here participants were asked to describe the contents of their dreams. This gives us richer and more interesting data, but such data are difficult to use for comparisons and are hard to analyse statistically.

IS THE RESEARCH ECOLOGICALLY VALID?

The research studied participants who went to sleep in a laboratory with electrodes stuck to their head. It is unlikely that this bears much relation to sleep in a normal environment! It is possible that being in such an artificial condition meant that their sleep was disturbed and if this was the case, the researchers would not have been studying normal sleep patterns. The participants were also woken up several times during the night and asked about their dreams. Again, this is unlikely

Fig. 4.9 Can an alarm clock ringing affect the content of our dreams?

☕ FOR CONSIDERATION

Dement and Kleitman's research suggests that external events (such as an alarm clock ringing) can affect the content of our dreams. Design an experiment to test this hypothesis.

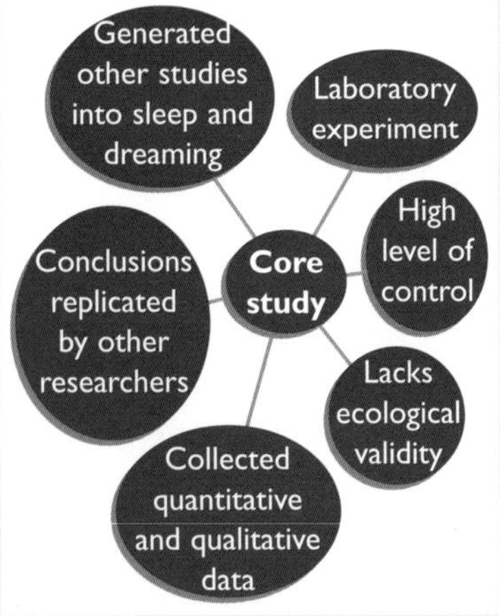

Fig. 4.10 Evaluating the core study

[Diagram: Core study — Generated other studies into sleep and dreaming; Laboratory experiment; High level of control; Lacks ecological validity; Collected quantitative and qualitative data; Conclusions replicated by other researchers]

to happen normally and may have had an effect on the way the participants slept. However, research conducted outside of the controlled conditions of the laboratory would have been unable to measure brain activity and eye movements in this way.

IS THE STUDY USEFUL?

The conclusions that were reached by Dement and Kleitman have been replicated by many other researchers. However, there is one methodological issue that should be considered. In relation to the first research question, Dement and Kleitman conclude that dreaming takes place in REM rather then non-REM sleep. What they have actually demonstrated is that dreams are recalled more often from REM rather than non-REM sleep and it may be that dreaming does occur in non-REM sleep but it is much harder to recall them.

When the research was first conducted, very little was known about the relationship between eye movements and dreaming and so Dement and Kleitman's research really did add new information to what was known about sleep. It is difficult, nearly 50 years later, to understand what a major breakthrough this study represented. The use of EEG to record brain activity whilst sleeping was also relatively new and it was not until research like this core study, that it became clear that dreams could be studied in an objective way. Dement and Kleitman's research generated very many other studies into sleep and dreaming and there have been many useful findings.

HOW IS INFORMATION RECEIVED BY THE BRAIN?

The brain is made up of two halves called **hemispheres**. The *left* hemisphere receives information from the *right* visual field and controls the *right* side of the body. The *right* hemisphere receives information from the *left* visual field and controls the *left* side of the body. The **corpus callosum** is a bundle of nerve fibres that connect the two hemispheres and this allows the two hemispheres to 'swap' data.

WHAT ARE THE FUNCTIONS OF THE TWO HEMISPHERES?

The two hemispheres have very different functions (see Fig. 4.11):
* The left hemisphere could be described as the 'words' hemisphere as this hemisphere controls the ability to speak, understand language and reason things out.
* The right hemisphere is the 'pictures' hemisphere and specialises in tasks such as drawing, spatial awareness (judging where you are in space) and intuitive tasks.

HOW WERE THE FUNCTIONS IDENTIFIED?

The language abilities of the left hemisphere were first identified in the nineteenth century by Broca and Wernicke.

In 1861, Broca published a case study of a patient who could only say the word 'tan', although his ability to understand language seemed normal. 'Tan' (as he is referred to in the case study) died shortly after admission to hospital and an autopsy showed an area of damage in the lower part of the left frontal lobe. Broca also identified eight similar cases and concluded that this area of the brain is responsible for the production of spoken language as damage to this area produces an aphasia (problem in the production and/or comprehension of language). Tan had a motor aphasia as he could understand speech but could not

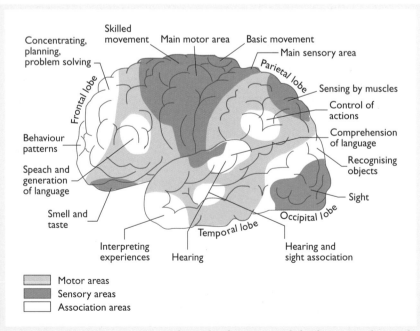

Fig. 4.11 *Where the functions of the brain are located*

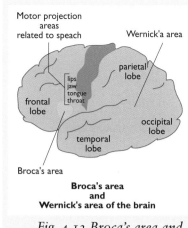

Fig. 4.12 *Broca's area and Wernicke's area*

produce speech. The work conducted by Broca led to this region of the brain becoming known as **Broca's area**.

In 1874, Wernicke reported on a number of patients suffering from a different type of aphasia. These patients could speak, although the content of their speech had little if anything to do with the conversation going on at the time. These patients appeared to have little understanding of words, could not respond to simple questions, repeat simple phrases or follow instructions. Autopsies revealed damage to the top of the left temporal lobe, a region of the brain now referred to as **Wernicke's area**.

Although the work of Broca and Wernicke has been refined, these basic findings are still valid ones and were the first scientific indication of hemisphere organisation. These findings demonstrate that the two hemispheres are not equivalent in terms of the cognitive tasks that they perform. It was not until the 1950s that testing procedures developed by Sperry allowed researchers to explore the different abilities of the hemispheres on a number of verbal and non-verbal tasks.

WHO WAS SPERRY WORKING WITH?

Sperry worked with epileptic patients. An epilephic attack is a violent and uncontrolled electrical discharge in the brain which causes disruption to normal brain functions. In some people, such attacks are barely noticeable, but in extreme cases they can cause collapse, tremor and loss of consciousness. Because the brain is such a good conductor of electrical impulses, the attack spreads rapidly and an attack beginning in one hemisphere will spread rapidly to the other hemisphere via the corpus callosum.

In the 1940s, an extreme solution to severe epilepsy was developed. The corpus callosum was cut, thus preventing the spread of an epileptic attack from one hemisphere to the other. Naturally this also resulted in the hemispheres being unable to transfer information between them. Given the scale of the brain damage caused by this operation, **'split-brain' patients** (as they became known) showed remarkably few side-effects and most gained significant relief from their epilepsy.

Green (1994) comments: 'Researchers in the 1940s were baffled as to what the corpus callosum might be doing in the normal brain, if cutting it had such minor effects. Some were reduced to proposing that it was simply there to hold the two hemispheres together!'

Sperry realised that the split-brain patients provided researchers with an opportunity to study the functions of the two hemispheres in ways which would never be possible experimentally.

Sperry's major contribution to this area of research was in the design of apparatus which allowed information to be sent to just one hemisphere. The core study described in the next section reports on the findings of Sperry's groundbreaking research in this area.

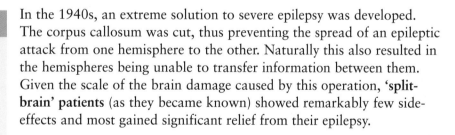

FOR CONSIDERATION

- The corpus callosum is the largest pathway in the brain comprising 250 million axons travelling across the brain and connecting sites in one hemisphere with equivalent sites in the other.
- No one would agree to have their corpus callosum severed for the purposes of research! The fact that a small number of people had had this operation to control their epilepsy made them extremely valuable research subjects.

SECTION 8 | SPERRY (1968): THE CORE STUDY

Fig. 4.13 Sperry

Fig. 4.14 Sperry's apparatus

QUOTE

'Instead of the normally unified single stream of consciousness, these patients behave as if they have two independent streams of conscious awareness, one in each hemisphere, each of which is cut off from and out of contact with the mental experiences of the other. In other words, each hemisphere seems to have its own separate and private sensations, its own perceptions; its own concepts; and its own impulses to act; with related volitional, cognitive and learning experiences. Following the surgery each hemisphere also has thereafter its own separate chain of memories that are rendered inaccessible to the recall processes of the other.' (Sperry, 1968)

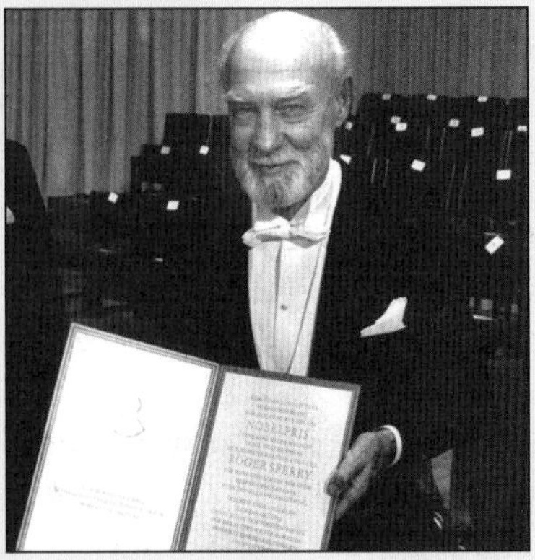

WHAT WAS THE AIM OF THE STUDY?

Sperry was attempting to study the functions of separated and independent hemispheres in the brain.

WHO DID SPERRY TEST?

The participants included 11 people who had already undergone surgery to sever their corpus callosum.

HOW WERE THE PARTICIPANTS TESTED?

Sperry used specially designed apparatus that allows information to be presented to just one hemisphere. The individual's vision is divided into the left and right visual fields and their hands are screened from their own view.

WHAT DID SPERRY FIND?

- If the visual fields are divided and one piece of information is sent to the left visual field (and so to the right hemisphere), it is only recognised again if seen by the same visual field. The right visual field (and left hemisphere) has never seen it before.
- Visual material shown to the right visual field (left hemisphere) can be described in speech and writing. If the same material is shown to the left visual field (right hemisphere) the participant insists that he did not see anything. However, if instead of asking the participant to tell you what he saw, he is asked to use his left hand to point to the object among a collection of other objects the participant is able to select accurately the item he has 'just insisted he did not see'.
- Even more interestingly, if a different figure is flashed to each hemisphere (for example a dollar sign to the left visual field and a question mark to the right visual field), and the participant is asked to draw what he has seen with his left hand, he will draw the figure seen in the left visual field. But if you ask him what he has drawn, he will tell you that he drew the object that appeared in the right half of the field. As Sperry notes: 'The one hemisphere does not know what the other hemisphere has been doing'.
- Objects put in the right hand can be readily described and named. Participants simply make wild guesses about objects put in their left hands and may even be unaware that anything at all is present. However, they can still select it correctly from a collection of other objects. Unlike a 'normal' person however, they can only do this with the same hand that the object was originally placed in. If two objects are placed one in each hand, each hand can then search for its own object but will in the process reject the object that the other hand is

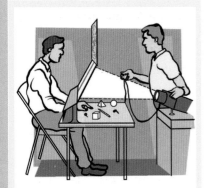

looking for. It is simply as if two separate people are working at the task.

Sperry and his team were fascinated to discover what goes on in the 'speechless' right hemisphere. Their results suggest that this hemisphere is capable of complex tasks although it is not able to express itself verbally. The research showed that the right (minor) hemisphere is able to perform the following:

- Select similar items to a target item (e.g. a watch rather then a clock) perform simple arithmetic operations.
- Understand both written and spoken words (e.g. if the word 'eraser' is flashed to the left visual field (right hemisphere) the subject can select an eraser from a collection of objects using the left hand but can't name it).
- If asked to select a piece of silverware, the left hand can select a fork, but the individual may well report that they have chosen a knife or a spoon. Both hemispheres heard the instruction but only the right hemisphere knows which item has been selected. The left (talking hemisphere) does not know the correct answer.
- It can understand fairly complex instructions (find something used to remove dirt – soap, find something inserted in slot machines – coin).
- It has appropriate emotional reactions (if nude photos were flashed to the right hemisphere the participant typically denies seeing anything but may blush or giggle suggesting that the picture was registered at some emotional level).

HOW DO THE PATIENTS MANAGE IN EVERYDAY LIFE?

Many of the problems described above do not arise in everyday life. They only arise when information is flashed for fractions of a second using complex apparatus that does not allow for eye movements which would automatically mean the material was in both visual fields. Many effects only occur when people are prevented from seeing their hands (which would allow information to go to both hemispheres) and many other effects are easily compensated for by speaking aloud which transfers much information to the minor hemisphere in a more indirect way.

THINKING LIKE A PSYCHOLOGIST – EVALUATING THE CORE STUDY

WHAT ARE THE STRENGTHS AND WEAKNESSES OF SPERRY'S METHOD?

Fig. 4.15 Brain surgery

Sperry conducted a **quasi-experimental** design. One weakness of this is that it does not give the researcher full control over the independent variable (whether someone had their corpus callosum severed). However, quasi-experimental designs allow researchers to investigate variables that are not able to be investigated in strict laboratory experiments. Sperry's research can be seen as similar to a collection of detailed case studies conducted with highly controlled and objective laboratory equipment and procedures. The major strength of Sperry's work is the techniques that he developed which allowed the functions of the two hemispheres to be studied in ways which had previously been impossible.

WAS THE SAMPLE REPRESENTATIVE?

FOR CONSIDERATION

Other researchers have continued Sperry's pioneering work. One of these is Gazzaniga (1977). Try to find out about this research.

Sperry had 11 participants who had already undergone surgery to sever their corpus callosum. This would be considered quite a small number in other types of studies, but it would not have been possible to find large numbers of people who had had this operation. There are two questions that need to be considered: first, are these 11 people representative of everyone who has had this operation; second, can the results of this study be used to tell us anything about the functioning of the 'normal' brain?

The results suggest that all the participants experienced very similar effects to each other and so it would be safe to conclude that anyone who had this operation would experience these effects. However, as Sperry did not control the independent variable in this study, he was not able to test these participants prior to the operation. It is possible that their brain functioning may have been atypical (different from the norm) before the operation and this would make drawing conclusions about the functions of the hemispheres in non-separated brains more difficult.

Fig. 4.16 Evaluating the core study

WHAT TYPE OF DATA WAS COLLECTED?

There are examples of both quantitative and qualitative data in this study. The majority of the data are quantitative as Sperry simply records whether something could be identified or not. These are the important data in this study as it is from them that Sperry is able to draw his conclusions about the different functioning of the two hemispheres. However, the results are illustrated with some revealing

qualitative examples of the experiences of the split-brain patients and this adds significantly to our attempt to understand the experiences of these people. For example, the description of patients giggling at nude photographs presented to their right hemisphere while denying that they have seen anything is far more revealing than simply reporting how many responded and under what conditions.

IS THE RESEARCH ECOLOGICALLY VALID?

In a sense, this research has very little ecological validity as the techniques that Sperry developed artificially separate the visual and tactile information received by the individual. It is difficult to think of a situation where this would happen in real life, and as we saw in the core study, split-brain patients have a number of simple strategies for coping in the real world that they were unable to use in laboratory conditions. On the other hand, ecologically valid research should be studying real problems and Sperry's research is looking at a naturally occurring variable (split brain as a result of the operation) and trying to understand exactly what effects this operation has on the individuals concerned.

IS THE RESEARCH USEFUL?

Sperry's work revealed important facts about the **lateralisation of functions** between the two hemispheres of the brain that had only been suggested by previous studies. There are many ways in which this knowledge could be applied to helping people cope with the effects of brain damage.

RAINE, BUCHSBAUM AND LACASSE (1997): BACKGROUND

HOW HAVE PSYCHOLOGISTS EXPLAINED AGGRESSIVE BEHAVIOUR?

There are many theories of aggression and it is outside the scope of this book to explore all of them. A few are outlined below.

The Frustration-Aggression theory (Dollard, 1939) proposes that aggression is an innate (inborn) response to any frustrating external stimuli.

Freudian theory proposes that aggression is the result of thanatos (the death instinct) which drives individuals towards their own self-destruction. Defence mechanisms cause the 'displacement' of aggressive urges outward. Freud describes aggression as building up naturally within us and requiring release. If this aggression is not released safely (through sport for example), it may eventually cause a dangerous violent outburst.

Fig. 4.17 Theories of aggressive behaviour

Social Learning theory, first put forward by Bandura and Walters in the 1960s, proposes that aggression is a learned behaviour, i.e., we learn to be aggressive through the processes of observation, imitation, shaping and reinforcement.

Ethology describes animal aggression as highly adaptive and necessary for survival.

Social psychology offers us several explanations of aggression. These include **conformity to social norms** and **deindividuation**.

Biological explanations of aggression include **genetic theories** which propose that the genetic make-up of certain people makes them more likely to be violent, **biochemical theories** point to factors such as raised levels of testosterone, and **neurological theories** suggest that certain brain areas, in particular the temporal lobes and the limbic system, may be involved in aggressive behaviour. It is possible that injury or damage to these areas might make a person aggressive. It is this approach to extreme acts of aggression (murder) that we will be looking at in the core study by Raine *et al*.

HOW CAN WE INVESTIGATE THE NEUROPHYSIOLOGY OF AGGRESSION?

In the past, it was often only possible to investigate links between neurophysiology and violent behaviour through animal studies (which may not be generalised to humans) or by autopsy. The development of brain scanning techniques has opened up a new opportunity for research in this area.

There are several types of brain scan:

- **Electroencephalography (EEG)** measures 'brain waves'. This has been described in the background to the core study by Dement and Kleitman (see page 78).
- **Magnetic resonance imaging (MRI)** aligns atomic particles in the body tissues by magnetism and then bombards them with radio waves. Different sorts of body tissues give off different signals and these signals can be converted into a 3D picture.
- **Positron emission tomography (PET)** identifies the brain areas that are working hardest by measuring their fuel intake. PET scans allow researchers to examine the relationship between activity in the brain and mental processes. PET works by measuring the level of metabolic activity occurring within the brain. Someone having a PET scan is first injected with a small amount of harmless radioactive material 'bonded' to a substance such as glucose. Since the brain's primary form of energy is glucose, the areas which are most active absorb more of it. The glucose is broken down by the brain, but the radioactive material is not, and as it decays it emits positively charged particles called positrons which are detected by the scan. This information is then fed into a computer which produces different coloured images of the level of activity occurring throughout the brain, with the different colours indicating different levels of activity.

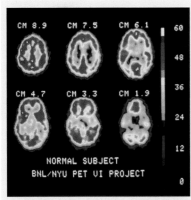

*Fig. 4.18 A PET scan
The core study by Raine, Bucksbaum and Lacasses uses PET scans.*

PET scans can be used to:

- provide images of what is going on in the brain *during* various *behaviours* (an advantage over other scanning techniques such as CAT and MRI scans)
- identify those areas of the brain that are active when we are *thinking* (e.g. different brain activity has been found in response to the instructions 'Move your right hand' and 'Think about moving your right hand')
- locate tumours and growths (to provide vital information about the likelihood of essential brain structures being damaged by surgery)
- reveal possible differences between the brains of people with and without psychological disorders (some differences have been found between the brains of schizophrenics and non-schizophrenics – supporting the idea that this disorder has a physical cause)
- explore differences between the sexes (Gur *et al.* (1995) showed that men have a more active metabolism than women in the primitive brain centres that control sex and violence).

RAINE, BUCHSBAUM AND LACASSE (1997): THE CORE STUDY

WHAT WAS THE AIM OF THE STUDY?

Its aim was to discover, using PET scans, whether there are brain abnormalities in murderers who plead not guilty by reason of insanity (NGRI).

WHO DID RAINE ET AL. TEST?

The experimental group consisted of 41 individuals charged with murder (or manslaughter). There were 39 men and two women and their average age was 34 years. The PET scans were to provide evidence for an NGRI defence, incompetence to stand trial or as evidence for diminished responsibility prior to sentencing.

The reasons for referral included:
- head injury or organic brain damage (23)
- schizophrenia (6)
- hyperactivity/learning disorders (3)
- epilepsy (2)
- affective disorder (2)
- passive – aggressive or paranoid personality disorder (2).

All of the participants were in custody at the time of the study and had been medication free for a two-week period prior to the PET scans. This was confirmed by urine testing.

The **control group** was formed by matching each individual in the NGRI group with someone of the same age and sex. The six schizophrenic NGRIs were further matched with six schizophrenics from a larger psychiatric sample being tested. Subjects with a history of head trauma, seizures or substance abuse were excluded and none was taking any medication.

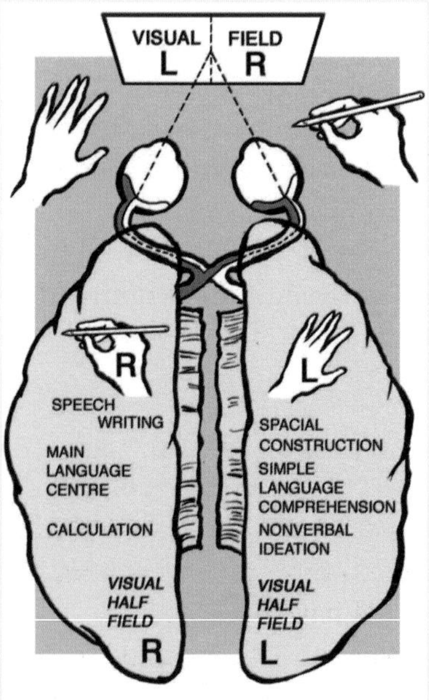

HOW WERE THE PARTICIPANTS TESTED?

Participants were injected with the tracer and monitored for a 32-minute period while they completed a continuous performance task (which measures target recognition accuracy). After the 32 minutes, the participants were transferred to the PET scanner room for scanning.

WHAT DID THE PET SCANS SHOW?

- Reduced glucose metabolism in prefrontal cortex, posterior cortex and corpus callosum.

Fig. 4.19 Raine

Fig. 4.20 The brain

- Abnormal asymmetries of activity (left lower than right) in the amygdala, thalamus and hippocampus.

 CD-ROM

The Physiological Approach: Web investigation: Raine

There were no differences between the groups on the continuous performance task and handedness and ethnicity had no effect. There was a slight difference between those NGRIs with a history of head trauma to have lower levels of activity in the corpus callosum than the other NGRIS.

What does this mean?

Raine explains that damage to the pre-frontal cortex can result in impulsivity, immaturity, altered emotionality, loss of self-control and the inability to modify behaviour. All of these may increase the likelihood of aggressive acts.

The amygdala is associated with aggressive behaviour and also the recognition of emotional stimuli such as a fearful expression on someone's face. Damage to the amygdala is associated with 'fearlessness'. The part of the limbic system made up of the amygdala, hippocampus and prefrontal cortex governs the expression of emotion. Together with the thalamus, these areas are also important in learning, memory and attention and the suggestion is made that abnormal functioning may lead to problems such as not being able to form conditioned emotional responses and the failure to learn from experiences.

KEY CONCEPT

- The amygdala has been associated with theory of mind. See the core study by Baron-Cohen, Leslie and Frith (page 30).
- See the core study by Sperry for more on the hemispheres (page 84).

Poor hemispheric transfer may mean that the right hemisphere (which generates negative emotions) may be less regulated by the right hemisphere than in controls.

WHAT ARE THE STUDY'S CONCLUSIONS?

Raine himself points out that this study has several limitations. Only the six schizophrenic participants were matched with psychiatric controls (people with the same mental illness who had not committed murder) and this could have been done for the whole group. He also points out that the study does not look at violent behaviour in general but at a very specific sub-group of violent behaviour and so we should be cautious about drawing conclusions about violence in general. PET scans are still being developed and some of the problems associated with these scans is discussed in the next section.

The results cannot be taken to indicate that violence is determined by biology alone and neither do they suggest that murderers pleading NGRI are not responsible for their actions. The results do not establish the cause (biological or environmental) of brain dysfunction, although they do suggest that murderers pleading NGRI have significantly different patterns of glucose metabolism in the brain and that these differences may make a person more likely to be violent. These points are discussed further in the next section.

THINKING LIKE A PSYCHOLOGIST – EVALUATING THE CORE STUDY

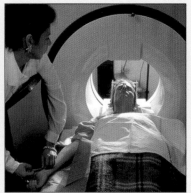

Fig. 4.21 Patient being prepared for PET scan

WHAT ARE THE STRENGTHS AND WEAKNESSES OF RAINE ET AL.'S METHOD?

This study was a **highly controlled laboratory (quasi) experiment** using very sophisticated equipment. However, there are some problems with PET scans and these include the fact that the generation of the images is a very complex process with the scope for errors. PET scans identify 'hotspots of activity', but these could be excitatory nerves (the 'on' switch) or inhibitory nerves (the 'off' switch). As the brain becomes practised at a task, the amount of activity declines and this means that activity seen on a scan may simply represent the brain processing something new. All of the above means that we should treat the data produced from a PET scan with caution. Finally, PET scans require an injection into the bloodstream of a radioactive marker. The dose is tiny but for safety reasons no one is allowed to have more than one scanning session (twelve scans) per year.

WAS THE SAMPLE REPRESENTATIVE?

This is a difficult question to answer! Was the sample representative of murderers? Was the sample representative of murderers claiming not guilty by reason of insanity (NGRI)? Would it even be possible to establish this? The matching by age and sex (and schizophrenia) is a strength of the study, but further matching by mental illness could have been used. It might also have been interesting to compare the brain activities of murderers claiming NGRI with murderers not claiming this, although this would raise very many ethical and practical issues. Finally, 41 participants in the experimental and control groups is a reasonable size sample for this kind of research.

WHAT TYPE OF DATA WAS COLLECTED?

The data collected were quantitative as the colours in the PET scans represent different levels of metabolic activity in the brain. PET scans will produce reliable data (in the sense that the PET scanner will measure metabolic activity consistently), but as we have already seen, there is scope for error in the interpretation of the data. The data represented metabolic activity during a continuous performance task and while it is certainly interesting to discover that murderers and non-murderers show different levels of activity, it is difficult to see how activity during a such a task can tell us anything about the reasons for someone committing a murder.

 FOR CONSIDERATION

Explain why Raine *et al.'s* study is best described as a quasi-experiment.

 FOR CONSIDERATION

Compare the sample size of this study with the sample size of the studies conducted by Sperry (see page 84) and by Dement and Kleitman (see page 78).

FOR CONSIDERATION

How could this kind of research be applied?

What practical or ethical implications might arise from the argument that people with certain patterns of brain activity were more likely to commit murder?

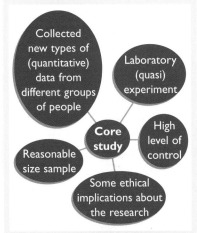

Fig. 4.22 Evaluating the core study

HOT EXAM HINT

You should be able to:
- describe the aim, sample, method and results of the study clearly (although you need not worry about detailed biological explanations)
- explain what differences were identified and what behaviours these differences might be associated with.

FOR CONSIDERATION

1 What are the ethical implications of this research? How might the results be used?
2 Evaluate the use of the continuous performance task in this study?
3 How many reasons can you think of for someone committing a murder? How many of these reasons would be 'biological' ones?
4 What other groups of people might it be to interesting to study in this way?

WAS THE STUDY REDUCTIONIST?

The study 'reduces' the behaviour of murder to a measure of metabolic activity in the brain. As Raine *et al.* would no doubt agree, murder is a complex act which is likely to be affected by a number of social and individual variables and cannot be explained simply in terms of metabolic activity. In support of the study, it could be argued that Raine *et al.* have identified a very important difference between the brains of murderers and non-murderers which will no doubt generate more research.

WHAT DOES THE STUDY TELL US ABOUT THE NATURE-NURTURE DEBATE?

It is difficult to draw conclusions about the causes of murder from this study. It is not possible to conclude that the differences in brain activity did cause the individuals to commit murder and the results definitely do not suggest that violence is determined by biology alone. Neither do the results tell us what caused the differences in brain activity in the first place and this could be genetic, biological or environmental.

IS THE STUDY ETHICAL?

The research itself does not appear to break any ethical guidelines, but there are **ethical implications**. If the results were taken by some to suggest that people with a particular pattern of brain activity were likely to commit murder, then all kinds of 'science fiction' scenarios could be imagined. This would overlap with the issue of social control.

IS THE RESEARCH USEFUL?

The ability to collect new types of data from different groups of people is always useful. Raine's work has established a potentially significant difference in the brains of murderers who are claiming that they are not guilty by reason of insanity. The comments made above clearly suggest that the results should be treated with caution, but there is no doubt that this kind of research will continue.

USEFUL RESOURCES

HOT EXAM HINTS

STRENGTHS OF THE PHYSIOLOGICAL APPROACH INCLUDE:

- It demonstrates a link between brain activity and cognitive processes (Dement and Kleitman, Raine).
- It uses highly controlled conditions and specialized techniques (Sperry, Raine).
- It contributes to our understanding of the nature-nurture debate (Raine).

WEAKNESSES OF THE PHYSIOLOGICAL APPROACH INCLUDE:

- It may be reductionist.
- Tasks may lack ecological validity.
- Some research breaks ethical guidelines (Schachter and Singer).
- Some research may have implications for social control (Raine).

CD-ROM

The Physiological Approach:
The human nervous system;
Personality and stress;
Stress and the workplace
Revision: Crosswords: Physiological

BOOKS

Gross, R. (2001) *Psychology: The Science of Mind of Behaviour*, Hodder & Stoughton, 4th edn.
This is an excellent general psychology textbook and chapters 4, 5, 7 and 10 will give you plenty of information on the topics covered in this section. Chapter 46 considers issues related to criminological psychology.

Carter, R. (1998) *Mapping the Mind*, Phoenix.
A wonderfully illustrated book covering many aspects of physiological psychology and including some fascinating case studies.

Dement, W. and Vaughn, C. (2000) *The Promise of Sleep*, Macmillan.
A fascinating book on sleep, including sections on dreaming, sleep disorders and sleep deprivation.

Other good books on physiological psychology include:
Green, S. (1994) *Principles of BioPsychology*, Laurence Erlbaum.
Temple, C. (1993). *The Brain: An introduction to the Psychology of the Human Brain and Behaviour*, Penguin.
Pinker, S. (1997) *How the Mind Works*, Penguin.

WEBSITES

Go to www.heinemann.co.uk/hotlinks and insert the code 670XP.
Look at the websites listed under Physiological: Useful websites.

CHAPTER **5**   THE SOCIAL APPROACH

THE CORE STUDIES

WHAT IS SOCIAL PSYCHOLOGY?

Social psychology looks at a range of behaviours that are primarily social in nature, that is, they occur between people or groups or people. Many of the topics investigated by social psychologists have direct relevance to many of the news stories occurring each day, such as prejudice and discrimination, helping behaviour and aggression. Social psychologists are interested in the effects that environments (or situations) have on people's behaviour and have studied factors affecting conformity and obedience.

THE CORE STUDIES

Milgram (1963)

This is one of the best known pieces of psychological research. It is a **laboratory study** of obedience to authority which produced some horrifying results. The study has been heavily criticised on ethical grounds.

Haney, Banks and Zimbardo (1973)

This study used a mixture of **experimental and controlled observation methods** to examine the effect of a 'mock' prison environment on ordinary people playing the roles of prisoners and guards.

Piliavin, Rodin and Piliavin (1969)

This is a **field experiment** which examined helping behaviour towards different types of victims.

Tajfel (1970)

This is a **laboratory experiment** which investigated the conditions under which discrimination would occur. Tajfel concludes that 'minimal' groups can produce feelings of in-group belonging and discrimination towards an out-group.

MILGRAM (1963): BACKGROUND

WHAT IS MEANT BY OBEDIENCE TO AUTHORITY?

Fig. 5.1 Stanley Milgram

65 IN TEST BLINDLY OBEY ORDER TO INFLICT PAIN

This headline appeared in the *New York Times* in 1963. It referred to an experiment conducted by psychologist Stanley Milgram into obedience to authority.

Gross (1992) defines obedience as 'complying with the demands of an authority figure' and states that 'Obedience has to do with the **social power** and **status** of an authority figure in a hierarchical situation'.

Milgram's study showed the horrifying extent to which ordinary people are willing to submit to those who they see as being in control.

WHAT WAS MILGRAM'S INTEREST IN OBEDIENCE TO AUTHORITY?

Milgram's interest stemmed from a deep fascination with Nazi Germany and the Holocaust. Being Jewish, he identified with the suffering of fellow Jews at the hands of the Nazis and felt some guilt that he had managed to avoid suffering a similar fate.

Milgram wanted to try to understand how the Holocaust could have happened. What he set out to test in his obedience study was one of the proposals put forward by historians to explain the behaviour of the Germans, that is, the 'Germans are different' hypothesis. This hypothesis suggests that Germans have a basic character defect that causes them to blindly obey figures of authority no matter what they are being asked to do. After completing his study, it had been Milgram's intention to repeat the experiment in Germany, but this became unnecessary due to the surprising results he obtained. He found that rather than being a flaw in German personalities, blind obedience was in fact a flaw in all, or at least most personalities.

HOW DID MILGRAM MEASURE OBEDIENCE TO AUTHORITY?

Milgram measured obedience to authority by asking a group of volunteers to administer electric shocks of increasing strength to another volunteer. This second volunteer was in fact an accomplice of the experimenter and the electric shocks were not real. The level of obedience was measured by how far up the scale of shocks the participants were willing to go.

QUOTE

'I should have been born in the German speaking Jewish community of Prague in 1922 and died in a gas chamber some 20 years later. How I came to be born in the Bronx Hospital [New York] I'll never quite understand.' (Letter from Milgram to schoolmate John Schaffer in 1958)

FOR CONSIDERATION

Is obedience necessarily a flaw? Can you think of any situations in which blind obedience would be a good thing?

CD-ROM

The Social Approach: Milgram's experiment

Fig. 5.2 Milgram's advert for volunteers

FOR CONSIDERATION

Milgram agreed to pay participants $4 for one hour of their time. They were to be paid as soon as they arrived at the laboratory, not after they had completed the experiment. What do you think may be the significance of this?

WHO WERE THE PARTICIPANTS?

Milgram tested 40 males, aged 20–50, drawn from New Haven and the surrounding community. The participants had a range of occupations and educational backgrounds. He obtained his sample by advertising in newspapers and by direct mail for volunteers to participate in a study of memory and learning at Yale University.

WHERE DID THE EXPERIMENT TAKE PLACE?

The experiment took place in the Psychology laboratories at Yale University. When the volunteers arrived at the university, they were greeted by the experimenter, dressed in a grey lab coat, and told that they were taking part in an experiment to investigate the effect of **punishment on learning**. They were introduced to another 'volunteer' (an accomplice of the experimenter) and were told that they would draw lots to see who would be the **teacher** and who would be the **learner**. This procedure was in fact rigged so that the volunteer always drew the role of teacher and the bogus volunteer the role of learner.

WHAT DID MILGRAM EXPECT TO FIND?

Before conducting the experiment, Milgram questioned various people about how they thought the participants would respond in the experiment. In particular, he questioned 14 senior Psychology students at Yale University, giving them full details of the procedure; he asked them to predict the behaviour of 100 hypothetical participants. They unanimously agreed that only an insignificant minority (0–3 per cent) would continue to the end of the shock range. Milgram also questioned fellow psychologists and the general response was that few, if any, would go beyond the 300-volt shock. Hence Milgram had not expected his participants to behave as they did and he and his colleagues were shocked at the results of the experiment.

MILGRAM (1963): THE CORE STUDY

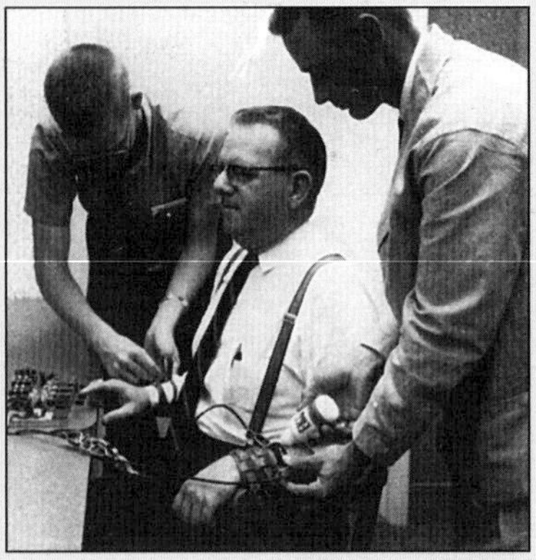

HOW WAS THE EXPERIMENT CARRIED OUT?

Fig. 5.3 *Learner strapped into an 'electric chair'*

The teacher witnessed the learner being strapped into an 'electric chair' with electrodes attached to his arms and heard him being told that the shocks would be painful but not harmful. The experimenter then took the teacher to an adjoining room where he was seated in front of an impressive 'shock generator' on which there were 30 switches clearly marked from 15 to 450 volts in 15-volt increments. Under the switches were labels such as 'slight shock', 'intense shock' and 'danger: severe shock'. The machine had working buzzers, lights and dials, all of a high quality to ensure an appearance of authenticity. To further convince the participants of its authenticity, they were given a sample shock of 45 volts before beginning the experiment.

WHAT WAS THE TEACHER'S ROLE?

The teacher was asked to read a list of word pairs to the learner, which he was to memorise. This list formed the basis of the learning task. The teacher then repeated the first word in the list giving four possible responses. The learner's task was to recall which of the four responses was originally paired with the word. If the answer was correct, the teacher moved on to the next word, but if it was incorrect, the teacher pressed the first switch on the generator to administer an electric shock to the learner. The teacher then moved on to the next word and continued in the same way, increasing the severity of the shock by 15 volts each time an incorrect answer was given.

WHAT WAS THE LEARNER'S ROLE?

The learner's responses to the task were predetermined, based on a schedule of approximately three wrong answers to one correct. Also pre-planned were the responses of the learner to the shocks, which were in fact, tape-recorded. The learner responded with increasing intensity to the shocks, starting with a loud cry, increasing to a shout of 'I can't stand the pain. Let me out', which by 300 volts became an agonised scream and a refusal to answer any more. After the 300-volt shock the learner made no further responses to either the shocks or the memory task.

HOW DID THE EXPERIMENTER ENCOURAGE THE TEACHER TO CONTINUE?

When, after the 300-volt shock, the learner failed to respond to the task, the experimenter instructed the teacher to treat this like a wrong answer and to continue shocking accordingly. If the teacher expressed any reluctance to continue, the experimenter responded with a

---

FOR CONSIDERATION

List the measures that Milgram used to ensure that the participants believed in the reality of the situation.

Fig. 5.4 *The shock generator used in Milgram's experiment*

FOR CONSIDERATION

One of the ethical guidelines that psychologists should follow is that participants in research should not be deceived. List the different ways in which Milgram deceived his participants.

The standardised series of prods consisted of the following:

1 Please continue.
2 The experiment requires that you continue.
3 It is absolutely essential that you continue.
4 You have no other choice, you must go on.

QUOTE

Milgram writes that his participants were observed to 'sweat, tremble, stutter, bite their lips, groan and dig their finger nails into their flesh'. Several also displayed 'nervous laughter' with 'full blown, uncontrollable seizures' in three cases, one 'so violently convulsive that it was necessary to call a halt to the experiment'.

FOR CONSIDERATION

Sixty-five per cent of participants showed total obedience. Why do you think they obeyed? Try to list all the factors that may have influenced their behaviour.

standardised series of prods encouraging him to continue. If the teacher failed to obey after the fourth prod, the experiment was terminated.

HOW OBEDIENT WERE THE VOLUNTEERS?

Of the 40 volunteers, all obeyed up to 300 volts, after which five refused to go any further. By 375 volts, a further nine had refused to continue. The remaining 26 continued to the end of the scale. Although the participants showed surprisingly high levels of obedience, they also displayed clear signs of discomfort and distress.

WHY DID THEY OBEY?

There are various factors that may have influenced the participants and contributed to the extreme levels of obedience seen in Milgram's experiment. They include the following:

- The location of the study at a prestigious university and the formal appearance of the experimenter.
- The apparent worthy purpose of the study.
- The fact that the learner had volunteered to participate.
- The teacher had made a commitment to the experimenter which was strengthened by payment.
- The teacher's role had occurred by chance; he could have been the one receiving the shocks.
- The experiment took place in a very closed setting with no one for the participants to discuss the situation with and little time for reflection.
- The teachers were told that the shocks were not dangerous.
- Up until shock 20, the learner was still participating in the experiment.
- The teacher experienced conflict between two deeply ingrained behaviour dispositions: not to harm others versus obedience to authority.

THINKING LIKE A PSYCHOLOGIST – EVALUATING THE CORE STUDY

WHAT ARE THE STRENGTHS AND WEAKNESSES MILGRAM'S METHOD?

The method used was a **laboratory experiment**. The main advantage that Milgram had with this method was the amount of control he had over the situation. He controlled what the participants saw, heard and experienced and was able to manipulate their behaviour through what they were exposed to. This method also allowed accurate measurement of variables and the clear standardised procedures meant that replication was possible.

The disadvantages of this method include low ecological validity and the influence of demand characteristics on the participants and it could be argued that they were behaving in the way that they thought was expected of them rather than producing natural behaviour. Milgram has also been heavily criticised regarding the ethics of this study (see below) .

WAS THE SAMPLE REPRESENTATIVE?

Milgram's sample was a **self-selected sample** of 40 males obtained through advertising. This could be regarded as being a biased sample as they were all male American citizens. They were also volunteers – the majority of the population is unlikely to volunteer to take part in research and those who do may be atypical (different from the norm) of the target population in some way. Hence there may be problems generalising from these results.

WHAT TYPE OF DATA WAS COLLECTED?

The data collected were quantitative in that they involved measuring participants' obedience level, numerically, in terms of how far up the voltage scale they were prepared to go. This type of data has the advantage of being easy to compare and to analyse statistically. However, Milgram included no qualitative descriptions of *why* the participants obeyed or how they felt during the experiment although there are a few brief descriptions of participants' behaviour during the experiment.

IS THE RESEARCH ECOLOGICALLY VALID?

As with all laboratory experiments, there are problems with Milgram's study regarding its ecological validity. It involved an extremely unusual task carried out under very artificial conditions

---

CD-ROM

The Social Approach:
Obedience in real life;
General issues in Milgram

FOR CONSIDERATION

In what ways might volunteers be different from those that do not volunteer?

FOR CONSIDERATION

What qualitative data would have been interesting? How could these data have been collected?

Fig. 5.5 Evaluating the core study

Fig. 5.6 Milgram's study stemmed from his horror of the Holocaust and Nazi Germany

HOT EXAM HINT

You should be able to:
- describe the aim, sample, method, results and conclusions of the study
- consider the ethics of this research in some detail
- draw your own conclusions as to whether or not Milgram was justified in conducting the research.

FOR CONSIDERATION

1 Consider the arguments for and against Milgram's study. Should it have been conducted?
2 How do you think the results may have differed if different samples had been used, for example women or children?
3 The study lacked ecological validity. Can you think of other methods of studying obedience that would have higher ecological validity? (Look up the Hofling (1966) study.)
4 Which authority figures in real life need to be obeyed?

and, as such, is likely to have produced very unnatural behaviour from the participants. This has implications for the extent to which we can generalise from the results to real life situations. It can be argued that the study tells us nothing about obedience in everyday life but simply shows us how obedient *these* people were, in *this* environment, performing *this* task.

IS THE STUDY ETHICAL?

Milgram's study is probably one of the most unethical pieces of psychological research ever conducted! It can be criticised in terms of almost all the British Psychological Society's Ethical Guidelines, including **informed consent, deception, right to withdraw** and **protection from harm.** However, in Milgram's defence, we can argue that he did not expect the participants to obey to the extent that they did or to find the task so stressful. He also conducted a thorough debriefing and follow-up monitoring of his participants. A survey conducted one year later revealed that 84 per cent of the participants were glad to have taken part and psychiatric examinations of them showed that none had suffered long-term harm.

WHAT DOES THE STUDY TELL US ABOUT INDIVIDUAL AND SITUATIONAL EXPLANATIONS OF BEHAVIOUR?

The individual explanation for the behaviour of the participants would be that it was something about them as people that caused them to obey, but a more realistic explanation is that the situation they were in influenced them and caused them to behave in the way that they did. Some of the aspects of the situation that may have influenced their behaviour include the formality of the location, the behaviour of the experimenter and the fact that it was an experiment for which they had volunteered and been paid.

IS THE STUDY USEFUL?

As stated earlier, the stimulus for the study was the Holocaust and this study has contributed significantly to the discussions regarding the behaviour of the Germans at this time. In particular, it provides strong evidence against the 'Germans are different' hypothesis. It also gives a valuable insight into the power of situations and of authority. The results suggest that we have a natural tendency to obey authority figures even when we feel that what we are being asked to do is morally wrong. However, the applications are restricted by methodological limitations such as low ecological validity and an unrepresentative sample.

HANEY, BANKS AND ZIMBARDO (1973): BACKGROUND

WHAT HAPPENS WHEN YOU PUT GOOD PEOPLE IN EVIL PLACES?

Fig. 5.7 Philip Zimbardo

Haney, Banks and Zimbardo addressed this question when they placed 24 law-abiding, intelligent, middle-class male volunteers in a 'mock' prison, assigning half of them to the role of **prisoners** and half to the role of **guards** with the instructions to 'maintain order'. The study was originally planned to run for two weeks but was abandoned after just six days due to the extreme reactions and deterioration of behaviour in both prisoners and guards. The study is often referred to as the Zimbardo prison study, as he was the main researcher.

WHY WAS THE STUDY CONDUCTED?

Part of the reason for the study was the shocking attempts at mass indoctrination by the Chinese during the Korean War in the early 1950s. Instead of merely containing enemy soldiers, the communists were actively trying to convert them to their 'side'. After the war was over, returning prisoners were extensively studied by psychologists and psychiatrists and a great deal of research was carried out, often financed by military authorities. This core study was sponsored by the Office of Naval Research and published in the journal *Naval Research Review*.

WHAT WAS THE AIM OF THE STUDY?

The aim of the study was to examine the effects of prison on its inhabitants. The focus was on trying to understand why prisons continually fail in terms of rehabilitation and as a deterrent to future crime and why they have such a dehumanising effect on both prisoners and guards. Zimbardo and his colleagues were aiming to test the **Dispositional hypothesis,** which proposes that the negative state of prisons is due to the nature of the people who run them, or the nature of the people who populate them, or both. Hence the dispositional hypothesis suggests that prisons are violent and brutal places because the guards are sadistic, uneducated and insensitive people and the prisoners are aggressive and have no regard for law, order or social convention. However, Zimbardo did not accept this explanation and felt that the prison environment itself was the strongest influence on the behaviour of its inhabitants (a situational hypothesis).

WHY A 'MOCK' PRISON?

Zimbardo wanted to separate the effects of the prison environment from the characteristics of its inhabitants and felt that the only way to achieve this was to set up a mock prison and place in it normal, stable, law-abiding citizens. This way they could examine the effects of the situation on the participants and attribute any negative behaviour to the situation rather than to the individuals.

HOW WAS THE PRISON DESIGNED?

Zimbardo consulted with prison personnel and ex-inmates when designing his prison in order to create as realistic a prison as possible. The aim was to create 'sufficient **mundane realism** to allow the role playing participants to go beyond the superficial demands of their assignment'.

However, differences necessarily existed between this and a real prison in that the researchers could not ethically allow violence, enforced homosexuality or racist practices to exist nor could they hold their participants for indefinite periods, all of which are typical features of real prisons.

WHERE DID THE STUDY TAKE PLACE?

The study took place at Stanford University where the prison was constructed in a 35-foot section of a basement corridor. Three small laboratory rooms (6 ft × 9 ft) were converted into cells, with all furniture removed and steel-barred doors to replace the original ones. The only furniture was three beds each with a sheet and pillow in each cell. A small, unlighted closet (2 ft × 2 ft × 7 ft) became the solitary confinement room known as 'The Hole'. A further small room formed the prison yard. Several rooms in an adjacent wing were used as guards' quarters. The cells were secretly bugged and at one end of the corridor was an observation screen equipped with video recorders.

Fig. 5.8 Laboratory rooms were converted into cells

WHO WERE THE PARTICIPANTS?

They were volunteers who answered a newspaper advert asking for males to participate in a 'psychological study of prison life' in return for $15 per day. All 75 respondents were given **diagnostic interviews** and **personality tests** to determine their physical and mental health, attitudes, family background and criminal involvement. A sample of 24 was selected as being the most physically and mentally stable, most mature and least involved in anti-social behaviour. They were all college students, largely of middle-class socio-economic status and white (with the exception of one Oriental participant). The study therefore began with an average group of healthy, intelligent, middle-class males.

Informed consent

All participants signed a contract agreeing to play the role of prisoner or guard for up to two weeks and guaranteeing a minimally adequate diet, clothing, housing and medical care. Also made clear was that the prisoners would be under surveillance and would have some of their basic rights suspended. Randomly determined by the flip of a coin, half of them were assigned to be guards and half prisoners.

FOR CONSIDERATION

Imagine spending time in The Hole. Try measuring out an area 2 ft × 2 ft and standing in it for five minutes. Now imagine yourself enclosed by walls, alone and in complete darkness!

Try also measuring out an area 6 ft × 9 ft. Imagine three people living in a room that size for 24 hours a day for almost a week!

HANEY, BANKS AND ZIMBARDO (1973): THE CORE STUDY

HOW DID THE STUDY BEGIN?

It all began on a quiet Sunday morning in August when a police car stormed through Stanford 'arresting' college students on suspicion of burglary or armed robbery, advising them of their rights, hand-cuffing them and searching them before carrying them off to the police station. Here they were fingerprinted, had an identity file prepared and were then placed in a detention cell. Throughout all this, the prisoners were unaware that this was part of the study and the police maintained a formal attitude, avoiding answering any questions relating their arrest to the study.

The prisoners were then blindfolded and taken to the mock prison. Here their degradation continued where they were stripped, sprayed with a delousing spray and made to stand alone and naked in the prison yard. They were eventually given a uniform, put into their cells and ordered to remain silent.

WHAT WAS THE GUARDS' ROLE?

The participants assigned to be guards attended an orientation meeting the day before the prisoners arrived. They were introduced to the experimenter, Zimbardo, who took on the role of superintendent, and a research assistant, who assumed the role of warden. They were told that their task was to 'maintain a reasonable degree of order within the prison necessary for its effective functioning' but were not specifically told how they should achieve this. They were warned to be prepared for unpredictable behaviour and to try and deal with it appropriately, but were clearly forbidden from using physical punishment or aggression. The warden informed the guards that they would work three-man 8-hour shifts and would be free to go home at all other times.

WHAT WAS THE PRISONERS' ROLE?

Three prisoners were randomly assigned to each cell. They were greeted by the warden who read them the rules of the prison, which they were to memorise. They were given an identity (ID) number, which would be used to refer to them in the prison. They were informed that they would be allowed two visiting periods per week in addition to the daily allowances shown in Fig. 5.9.

Three times a day all prisoners were to be lined up for a 'count', the purpose of which was to ascertain that all prisoners were present and to test them on their ID numbers and the rules.

FOR CONSIDERATION

Consider the psychological consequences of the 'arrest' and admission procedure. How do you think the prisoners felt as they sat silently in their cells?

CD-ROM

The Social Approach:
The Stanford Prison simulation

Fig. 5.9 A prisoner's daily allowance

WHAT DID THEY WEAR?

Both prisoners and guards were issued with uniforms, the purpose of which was to promote feelings of anonymity, to enhance group identity and reduce individual uniqueness. The guards' uniform was intended to convey a military attitude, suggesting control and power, while the prisoners' uniform was intended to be emasculating (to make the prisoner feel powerless) and humiliating and to suggest dependence and subservience.

WHAT WERE THE RESULTS?

At first, both prisoners and guards were unsure of how to behave. The prisoners did not take their roles seriously and the guards were feeling out their roles, unsure of how to assert their authority over the prisoners.

On the second day, the prisoners rebelled and locked themselves in their cells. The guards were very angry and, having sent for reinforcements, they forced the prisoners out of their cells using fire extinguishers. To avoid further rebellion, they decided to use psychological tactics to divide and so weaken the prisoners. They set up a privileges cell in which, initially, those least involved in the rebellion were placed. In order to confuse the prisoners, they later replaced these prisoners with the ring-leaders of the rebellion. This made the prisoners suspicious of each other and broke down any solidarity. From this point on, the behaviour of the guards became increasingly negative and aggressive and the punishments became more and more inhumane and humiliating. Soon, all rights became privileges to be earned. The worst instances of abuse occurred in the middle of the night when the guards thought the researchers were not watching.

From the quashing of the rebellion, the prisoners' behaviour also became more negative. Zimbardo described the deterioration of the prisoners as **pathological prisoner syndrome.** They learned very early on that the guards had all the power, and as the social cohesion broke down and the guards stepped up their aggression, the prisoners became more passive and dependent. They very soon developed feelings of helplessness and, as early as the second day, they started displaying extreme emotional reactions including depression, crying, rage, acute anxiety and psychosomatic rashes (caused by their mental or emotional condition rather than physical factors).

As a result of these extreme reactions five prisoners had to be released from the 'prison' early and the entire study was terminated after just six days.

THINKING LIKE A PSYCHOLOGIST – EVALUATING THE CORE STUDY

WHAT ARE THE STRENGTHS AND WEAKNESSES OF ZIMBARDO ET AL.'S METHOD?

The method is not clear-cut. Zimbardo refers to it as an **experiment** with the independent variable of assignment to either prisoner or guard and the hypothesis that assignment to guard or prisoner will result in significant differences in behaviour. However, it could also be described as a controlled observation as it involved recording spontaneously occurring behaviour under conditions contrived by the researcher. The main advantage of either of these methods is the researcher's control over the variables. The weaknesses can include low ecological validity and the influence of demand characteristics, which are discussed further below. There can also be ethical problems.

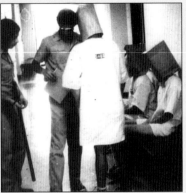

Fig. 5.11 Zimbardo's prison experiment

WAS THE SAMPLE REPRESENTATIVE?

The sample consisted of 24 volunteers who were predominantly white, middle-class, male students. This is clearly a biased sample as all the participants are the same gender, age, ethnic group and of similar educational and social backgrounds. Hence it would be difficult to generalise the results of this study to other, different groups in society.

CD-ROM

The Social Approach: Conformity in daily life

WHAT TYPE OF DATA WAS COLLECTED?

The data collected were both qualitative and quantitative. The qualitative data included details of transactions between groups of participants observed directly and recorded on video and audiotapes. Also collected were daily guard shift reports and post experimental interviews. The quantitative data were gained from personality and mood questionnaires. Hence the researchers had numerical data that they could compare and analyse and also detailed, descriptive information.

IS THE RESEARCH ECOLOGICALLY VALID?

There are two arguments regarding the ecological validity of this study. One is that it has high ecological validity because the prison environment in which the study takes place is very realistic and that the participants believed in the situation and displayed realistic behaviour. The other side of the argument is that the study lacks ecological validity because it is not a real prison, but an artificial environment created for an experiment and that the participants were simply responding to demand characteristics and acting out a role.

FOR CONSIDERATION

Which of these explanations do you favour? How would you support your decision?

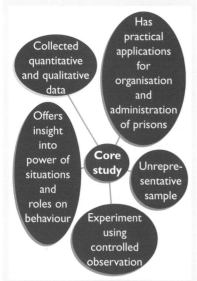

Fig. 5.12 Evaluating the core study

WHAT DOES THE STUDY TELL US …

About individual and situational explanations of behaviour?

The individual explanation for the behaviour of the participants would be that the guards behaved in the way that they did because they were naturally cruel and sadistic people and that the prisoners were naturally subservient and weak. However the fact that they were all initially screened and found to be similar in terms of mental and physical health and stability argues against this explanation, as does the fact that they were randomly allocated to the roles of prisoner and guard.

A more convincing explanation is that they behaved in the way that they did because of the situation they were in. *This would support the initial hypothesis* proposed by Zimbardo that the social environment created in prisons is what has the negative and destructive effect on its inhabitants.

About reinforcement?

A further explanation for the behaviour of the participants can be described in terms of reinforcement. The escalation of aggression and abuse by the guards could be seen as being due to the **positive reinforcement** they received both from fellow guards and in terms of how good it made them feel to have so much power.

Similarly, the prisoners could have learned through **negative reinforcement** that if they kept their heads down and did as they were told, they could avoid further unpleasant experiences.

IS THE RESEARCH USEFUL?

As the aim of the study was to examine the effect of prison on its inhabitants, the obvious real life applications are to the organisation and administration of real prisons. Following the research, Zimbardo proposed changes to prisons and to guard training, but his suggestions were not taken up and, in fact, prisons in the USA have been radically reformed in the last 25 years to make them less humane! However, testimony about the research influenced Congress to change one law so that juveniles accused of federal crimes cannot be housed before trial with adult prisoners because of the likelihood of violence against them. The study also gives a valuable insight into the power of situations and roles on behaviour.

PILIAVIN, RODIN AND PILIAVIN (1969): BACKGROUND

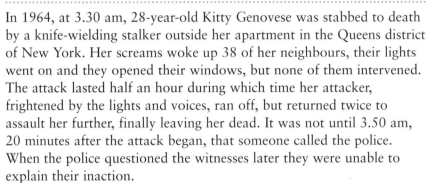

IS THE 'GOOD SAMARITAN' A THING OF THE PAST?

In 1964, at 3.30 am, 28-year-old Kitty Genovese was stabbed to death by a knife-wielding stalker outside her apartment in the Queens district of New York. Her screams woke up 38 of her neighbours, their lights went on and they opened their windows, but none of them intervened. The attack lasted half an hour during which time her attacker, frightened by the lights and voices, ran off, but returned twice to assault her further, finally leaving her dead. It was not until 3.50 am, 20 minutes after the attack began, that someone called the police. When the police questioned the witnesses later they were unable to explain their inaction.

More recently, in Britain in 1995, headmaster Philip Lawrence went to the aid of one of his pupils who was being bullied by youths from another school and was stabbed and killed by one of them.

These are two contrasting examples of **bystander behaviour**. In the Kitty Genovese case her neighbours showed **bystander apathy** and did nothing when help was needed, but Philip Lawrence intervened and paid with his life because he was not prepared to stand by and do nothing when someone needed help.

WHAT DOES RESEARCH TELL US ABOUT BYSTANDER BEHAVIOUR?

Much research has been conducted into the behaviour of bystanders and has examined the conditions under which people are most and least likely to give help. One finding is that people are more likely to help if they are alone than if there are others present.

Darley and Latane (1968) conducted a laboratory experiment where participants were asked to hold conversations with other participants through an intercom system and headphones. During the discussions they heard one of the participants having an epileptic seizure. The results showed that those who believed that other witnesses had heard the victim were less likely to seek help for him.

Latane and Rodin (1969) confirmed this finding in an experiment where participants in a waiting room heard a female fall and cry out in an adjoining room. Participants were significantly slower to respond and offer assistance when there were other people in the room than when they were alone.

Fig. 5.13 Bystander behaviour

HOW ARE THESE RESULTS EXPLAINED?

Darley and Latane put forward the **Diffusion of Responsibility hypothesis**, which proposes that as the number of bystanders increases, the likelihood that any individual will help decreases. It is thought that the more people there are present, the more there are to share the responsibility of helping, so that each individual's responsibility is lessened or diffused. In the Kitty Genovese case, as in the experiments above, the participants' responsibility to act was diffused by the presence of others and they assumed that someone else had taken action.

HOW DID PILIAVIN ET AL. STUDY BYSTANDER BEHAVIOUR?

The studies described above are laboratory experiments which have the advantage of greater control of variables by the experimenters but the disadvantage of low ecological validity. Piliavin *et al.* decided to conduct a field experiment, which provided a far more realistic arena in which to study bystander behaviour.

WHERE DID THE STUDY TAKE PLACE?

The study took place on the express trains of the New York Eighth Avenue Independent Subway where emergency situations were staged by the experimenters during the approximately $7\frac{1}{2}$-minute express run between 59th street and 125th street stations. This took place on weekdays between 11 am and 3 pm during the period 15 April to 26 June 1968. Trains A and D were selected because they made no stops between these two stations, thus providing the experimenters with a captive audience for $7\frac{1}{2}$ minutes!

FOR CONSIDERATION

Are there any ethical problems with such a 'captive' sample?

Fig. 5.14 The experiment took place in the New York Subway

PILIAVIN, RODIN AND PILIAVIN (1969): THE CORE STUDY

WHO CONDUCTED THE EXPERIMENT?

The experiment was conducted by 16 Columbia General Studies students, aged 24–35, divided into four teams of two males and two females. The males took on the roles of **victim** and **model** and the females recorded data. Of the victims, three were white and one black and all were identically dressed in jackets and trousers. The models were all white.

WHO WERE THE PARTICIPANTS?

The **unsolicited** participants were the 4,450 passengers who travelled on the train during this period. The sample included approximately 45 per cent black people and 55 per cent white people. There was an average of 43 people in each car with approximately eight in the critical area where the emergency took place.

WHAT WAS THE EMERGENCY?

The emergency consisted of the victim, who always stood at the pole in the centre of the carriage, staggering forward and collapsing. Until receiving help, he remained lying on his back on the floor staring up at the ceiling. If the victim received no help by the time the train slowed to a stop, the model helped him to his feet. When the train stopped the team would disembark and proceed to another platform to board a train going in the opposite direction for the next trial. Six to eight trials were run each day.

WHAT WERE THE DIFFERENT CONDITIONS OF THE EXPERIMENT?

The nature of the emergency situation varied according to the following factors:
- type of victim (drunk or ill)
- race of victim (black or white)
- presence or absence of model
- position and speed of response of model.

In the 'drunk' condition the 'victim' smelled of alcohol and carried a liquor bottle in a brown bag. In the 'ill' condition the 'victim' carried a black cane and appeared sober. In all other respects the 'victims' behaved identically.

The 'model' stood either in the critical area or near the critical area and offered assistance either after 70 seconds or after 150 seconds or did not offer help at all. When he provided assistance, he raised the

Fig. 5.15 The 'victim' lies waiting for help

'victim' to a sitting position and stayed with him for the remainder of the trial.

WHAT DID THE OBSERVERS RECORD?

The two female observers sat in the adjacent area and recorded the following information for each trial:
- gender, race and location of every passenger in the critical area
- time taken for first passenger to offer help
- total number of passengers who helped
- gender, race and location of every helper
- time taken for first passenger to offer help after the 'model' had assisted
- movement of any passengers out of the critical area
- spontaneous comments made by passengers.

WHAT WERE THE RESULTS?

The frequency of help received by the 'victim' was impressive and surprised the experimenters, bearing in mind the results of previous research into helping behaviour. The results were analysed and examined in terms of who received help, by whom and by how many, as well as how many people left the area or made spontaneous comments. Also examined was the Diffusion of Responsibility hypothesis. The general findings were as follows:
- The 'cane victim' received spontaneous help 95 per cent of the time compared to 50 per cent for the 'drunk victim'. This pattern was the same for both black and white 'victims'.
- Ninety per cent of the spontaneous first helpers were male even though only 60 per cent of the people in the critical area were male.
- There was no significant difference in the number of white and black spontaneous helpers.
- There was a slight tendency towards same-race helping, particularly in the 'drunk' condition.
- On 60 per cent of the trials where the 'victim' received help, he received it from more than one helper. This was the case for both black and white 'victims' and for both 'cane' and 'drunk' conditions.
- During the 103 trials, a total of 34 people left the critical area, but this occurred mainly in the 'drunk' condition.
- More spontaneous comments were made in the 'drunk' condition. The comments generally tended to be an attempt to justify or gain support for inaction.
- *There was no evidence to support the Diffusion of Responsibility hypothesis.* In contrast, the response times were consistently faster when there were seven or more people present compared to when there were three or less present.

FOR CONSIDERATION

Think about the ethics of this type of observation. Is it right to observe people and record their behaviour without their knowledge?

CD-ROM

The Social Approach:
Piliavin

FOR CONSIDERATION

The recorded spontaneous comments, made mainly by women, included the following:
- 'It's for men to help him.'
- 'I wish I could help him – I'm not strong enough.'
- 'I never saw this kind of thing before – I don't know where to look.'
- 'You feel so bad that you don't know what to do.'

THINKING LIKE A PSYCHOLOGIST – EVALUATING THE CORE STUDY

WHAT ARE THE STRENGTHS AND WEAKNESSES OF PILIAVIN ET AL.'S METHOD?

The method used was the **field experiment**. The main strength of this method is that it has high ecological validity and demand characteristics are unlikely to influence the participants. The weaknesses include the lack of control over the environment and the possibility of bias from extraneous variables. The lack of control also makes replication difficult. The field experiment can also have specific ethical problems, which are discussed in relation to this study below.

WAS THE SAMPLE REPRESENTATIVE?

The sample consisted of the 4,450 passengers using that particular train, 45 per cent of whom were black and 55 per cent white. This is a good-sized sample that is likely to be fairly representative of the American public. However the sample is restricted to the people who were using *that* train at *that* time.

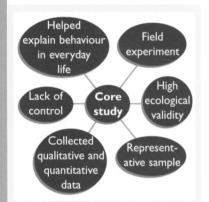

Fig. 5.16 Evaluating the core study

WHAT TYPE OF DATA WAS COLLECTED?

The data gathered were both qualitative and quantitative. The quantitative data included the number and type of passengers who helped as well as the time taken to offer assistance. The qualitative data came from the spontaneous comments made by the passengers. Both types of data are valuable in building up a full picture of what happened and why. The quantitative data allowed for comparisons and statistical analysis and the qualitative data provided some of the thoughts and feelings of the people involved perhaps providing explanations for why they did or did not help.

IS THE RESEARCH ECOLOGICALLY VALID?

As the study took place in a real life environment and the participants were unaware that they were part of a study, the ecological validity is very high. Hence, the behaviour displayed by the participants is likely to be their natural behaviour and the way in which they would behave in other situations.

Fig. 5.17 Participants were not informed that the collapse was staged

IS THE STUDY ETHICAL?

The ethical problems include the fact that the participants' consent was not gained and that they were deceived regarding the staged collapse and the identities of the researchers on the train. There is also a

FOR CONSIDERATION

When you conduct observations how will you ensure that your observations are reliable?

HOT EXAM HINT

You should be able to:
- describe the aim, sample, method, results and conclusions of the study
- describe the strengths and weaknesses of field experiments and of observational methods.

FOR CONSIDERATION

1 Considering the ethical criticisms of this study, should it have been conducted?

2 Why do you think the results of this study differ from those of Darley and Latane (1968) and Latane and Rodin (1969) in terms of the Diffusion of Responsibility hypothesis? What are the differences between these studies that may explain the differing results?

3 What are the problems with conducting psychological research in the everyday world?

4 What other methods could be used by psychologists to study bystander behaviour?

problem regarding invasion of privacy in that the participants were unaware that they were being observed and that data were being recorded about their behaviour.

WHAT DOES THE STUDY TELL US ABOUT RELIABILITY?

Reliability refers to the consistency of a measure and one aspect of reliability relevant to studies involving observations is how consistent different observers are when recording information on the same event, that is, inter-rater reliability. The reliability of this study was increased by the fact that there were two independent researchers observing and recording data. Hence they were able to measure inter-rater reliability.

IS THE RESEARCH USEFUL?

The study is a good example of where psychological research can be used to explain behaviour in everyday life. The fact that it is a field experiment with high ecological validity using a large sample makes the results highly applicable to other situations and environments, and useful in terms of explaining and predicting how people are likely to behave when faced with an emergency situation in real life. The study also provides strong evidence against the Diffusion of Responsibility hypothesis, which was supported by previous bystander research.

PREJUDICE
A fixed attitude, usually negative, towards someone on the basis of their membership of a particular category or group.

DISCRIMINATION
The behavioural expression of prejudice.

AUTHORITARIAN PERSONALITY
An individual who is overly respectful of authority and intolerant and hostile towards any individuals or groups who are different to the norm.

Fig. 5.18 In-group and out-group

KEY DEFINITIONS

IN-GROUP
A group that you consider yourself to be a member of.

OUT-GROUP
A group that you do not consider yourself to be a member of.

WHAT CAUSES PREJUDICE AND DISCRIMINATION?

This question has occupied the minds of politicians, historians, sociologists, psychologists and countless other groups for centuries. Some of the most extreme and well-known examples of **prejudice** and **discrimination** include the racial discrimination commonly seen in the USA and the religious discrimination found in Northern Ireland. However, prejudice and discrimination exist in all societies in some form or other and many people have been the victims of it. Therefore, discovering the causes of these destructive and anti-social features of our societies is a very important challenge and much research has been done in this area. Historians, sociologists and psychologists have all suggested theories concerning the origins of prejudice and discrimination.

WHAT ARE THE PSYCHOLOGICAL EXPLANATIONS FOR PREJUDICE AND DISCRIMINATION?

The psychological theories include explanations at individual and group levels. The individual explanation focuses on personality and suggests that individuals are prejudiced because they have a particular personality type known as the **authoritarian personality.**

The group explanation suggests that the existence of groups is what causes prejudice and discrimination. We are all members of some groups but not others and we naturally favour our **in-group** and are prejudiced against any **out-groups** that we are not members of. Group explanations of prejudice and discrimination include Sherif's **Realistic Group Conflict theory** and Tajfel's **Social Identity theory.**

Realistic Group Conflict theory

This theory suggests that prejudice develops when two groups are in conflict with each other because they are both competing for the same thing.

In 1961, Sherif *et al.* demonstrated how competition between groups could develop into prejudice. They studied a group of boys attending a summer camp. The boys were divided into two groups and were staying in different huts. In the first stage of the study, the two groups worked separately, but in the second stage, the researchers introduced an element of competition between them. Very quickly, the boys developed a strong team spirit that rapidly developed into hostility towards the other group. As the study went on, the boys developed an increasingly negative attitude towards the other group, which presented

Fig. 5.19 A minimal group

itself in both prejudiced attitudes and discriminatory behaviour towards them as well as a sense of in-group solidarity and superiority.

The Realistic Group Conflict theory proposes that the cause of prejudice and discrimination is the existence of different groups who are in conflict or competition with each other.

Social Identity theory

In contrast to Sherif's theory, Tajfel proposed that the mere existence of different groups is enough to create in-group favouritism and out-group prejudice. The theory suggests that when we become a member of a group it changes our perceptions of ourselves and we begin to identify with other members of that group and see ourselves as similar to them. In the same way, we begin to see members of other groups as different to us. These intra-group similarities and inter-group differences become more and more exaggerated.

The theory also proposes that our social identity is tied in with our group membership and that the position our group holds in society determines our self-esteem, or how we feel about ourselves. This leads us into making group comparisons and in order to raise our self-esteem, we see our group as being superior to others and we maximise the differences between our group and others.

Tajfel suggests that groups will compete even when there is no objective reason for doing so, and where the only aim is a positive self-identity, and that this is what leads to in-group favouritism and out-group prejudice and discrimination.

WHY WAS THE STUDY CONDUCTED?

To demonstrate his theory, Tajfel set up a series of studies known as the **minimal group** experiments. In these experiments he created the most minimal group situation possible – the mere recognition of two groups. There was no history to the group membership, no shared interests, no interaction between group members and personal rewards or outcomes were not dependent upon behaviour to other group members.

WHAT WAS THE AIM OF THE STUDY?

The aim of the study was to demonstrate that the mere knowledge of the existence of another group, of which the participant is not a member, is enough to create in-group favouritism and discrimination against the out-group. Tajfel conducted two separate experiments as part of the study.

TAJFEL (1970): THE CORE STUDY

THE GROUPS FOR EXPERIMENT 1

In the first experiment the boys were told that the experimenters were interested in visual judgements. Forty clusters of varying numbers of dots were flashed on to a screen and the boys were asked to estimate and record how many there were in each cluster. They were then told that they had either over or under estimated the number of dots. The experimenters then asked the boys to take part in another experiment and that, for convenience, they would be placed into groups according to whether they were over or under estimators. In fact, they were assigned to groups completely at random, with half in each group.

WHAT WERE THE PARTICIPANTS ASKED TO DO?

The boys were asked to complete a task that involved giving rewards and penalties in the form of small amounts of money to other boys. They would not know the identity of the boys they were rewarding or penalising but would know which group they belonged to. It was stressed that at no time would they be awarding money to themselves. The boys were placed individually in cubicles and were given a booklet to complete. The booklet contained a series of matrices consisting of eight boxes containing two numbers each.

THE DIFFERENT TYPES OF MATRICES

The participants had to respond to three different types of matrices offering one of the following choices:
- In-group choices – where top and bottom rows were both labelled as awarding money to members of their own group.
- Out-group choices – where top and bottom rows were both labelled as awarding money to members of the other group.
- Inter-group choices – where one row was labelled as awarding money to a member of their own group and the other row was labelled as awarding money to a member of the other group.

THE POSSIBLE RESPONSE STRATEGIES

The boys could have opted for three different strategies:
- Maximum joint profit – choosing the box with the highest total amount in each time so that, as a whole group, they got the most money out of the experimenters.
- Maximum fairness – choosing the box with near equal amounts in top and bottom rows so that each boy received the same amount.
- Inter-group discrimination – choosing the box that gave the most money to a member of his own group and the least amount to a member of the other group.

FOR CONSIDERATION

The participants were 64 boys, aged 14–15, from a Bristol comprehensive school. They came to the laboratory in groups of eight, with all the boys in each group coming from the same house and the same form at school, so they knew each other well.

23	22	21	20	19	18	17	16
5	7	9	11	13	15	17	19

Fig. 5.20 Example of a matrix in the first experiment

The numbers on the top row were amounts to be awarded to one person and the numbers on the bottom were amounts to be awarded to another person. Each row was labelled: *either* 'These are rewards and penalties for member number ... of your group' *or* 'These are rewards and penalties for member number ... of the other group'.

The participants were instructed to choose and mark a box from each matrix. At the top of each page was a reminder of the group that the participant was in.

FOR CONSIDERATION

Look at the sample matrix shown in Fig. 5.20. If this were an inter-group matrix where the top row was to be awarded to an in-group member and the bottom row to a member of the out-group, work out which box would give the following:

a maximum joint profit
b maximum fairness
c inter-group discrimination.

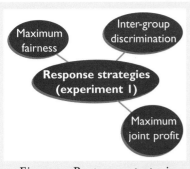

Fig. 5.21 *Response strategies for experiment 1*

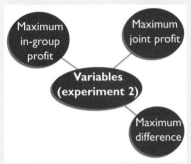

Fig. 5.22 *Variables for the second experiment*

Fig. 5.23 *Example of a matrix in the second experiment*

WHAT WERE THE RESULTS?

In both the in-group and out-group choices, the participants tended to opt for maximum fairness. However, in the inter-group choices, the boys showed clear inter-group discrimination in that they gave significantly more money to members of their own group than to members of the other group. These findings were consistent for all eight separately tested groups. In order to validate these results and analyse them further, Tajfel conducted a follow-up experiment.

HOW WAS THE SECOND EXPERIMENT RUN?

This experiment was similar to the previous one in that a sample of boys was randomly divided into groups, this time on the pretence that they had been divided according to a preference for paintings by Klee or Kandinsky. As in the first experiment, they were asked to complete booklets containing similar matrices, which again would result in them awarding money to other boys. However, the focus of this experiment was in assessing the relative weight of some of the variables that may influence the boys' decisions. In this experiment the researchers looked at three variables:

- maximum joint profit (MJP) – the largest possible joint award to both people
- maximum in-group profit (MIP) – the largest possible award to a member of the in-group.
- maximum difference (MD) – the largest possible difference in gain between a member of the in-group and a member of the out-group, in favour of the in-group.

WHAT WERE THE RESULTS?

The results showed that the boys typically ignored the maximum joint profit strategy and opted instead for the maximum in-group profit and the maximum difference. In situations where maximum in-group profit was combined on a matrix with maximum joint profit, where the out-group was getting more than the in-group (as in box 23/29 in Fig. 5.23), the boys tended to choose the maximum difference response (box 11/5), even though it meant their group gaining less money. The boys showed clear and blatant in-group favouritism and out-group discrimination. This pattern was also seen in the in-group and out-group matrices where the in-group choices were consistently nearer the maximum joint profit than were the out-group choices.

THINKING LIKE A PSYCHOLOGIST – EVALUATING THE CORE STUDY

WHAT ARE THE STRENGTHS AND WEAKNESSES OF TAJFEL'S METHOD?

Tajfel used the laboratory experiment method of research which had the advantage of enabling him to control the environment in terms of what the participants experienced, including the information and instructions given to them, and ensure that no other factors could influence their behaviour. Manipulation of the environment in this way enables **cause and effect relationships** to be indicated and the use of standardised procedures makes it possible to replicate the study.

The main disadvantage of this method is the lack of ecological validity which is discussed further below.

WAS THE SAMPLE REPRESENTATIVE?

The sample could be considered to be a biased one as the participants were all male, of similar age and from one particular school in one particular area of the country. It is difficult to see how these results could be generalised to other groups such as females, other age groups or people from other geographical areas. It could also be argued that these teenage boys were simply displaying the competitiveness typical of boys of this age and not discrimination.

WHAT TYPE OF DATA WAS COLLECTED?

The data generated were **quantitative** in that the researchers calculated the number of participants who selected the different options in the matrices. The data allowed for comparisons to be made and statistical analysis to be carried out. The study provided no qualitative data describing how the boys behaved or why they made the choices they did.

IS THE RESEARCH ECOLOGICALLY VALID?

The study can be criticised in terms of its low ecological validity. It involved an unusual task performed in an artificial environment and it could be argued that it produced unnatural behaviour on the part of the participants. There is also a strong possibility that they were influenced by the demand characteristics of the situation and acted in the way that they thought was expected of them.

☕ FOR CONSIDERATION

How do you think using a different sample might have affected the results?

How could the researchers have collected qualitative data in this experiment?

💿 CD-ROM

The Social Approach: Blue Eyes, Brown Eyes

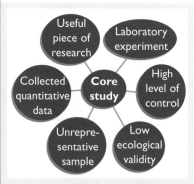

Fig. 5.24 Evaluating the core study

WHAT DOES THE STUDY TELL US ...

About reductionism?

Discrimination is clearly a very complicated human behaviour with many factors influencing it, and a criticism of Tajfel's study is that he has reduced this complex psychological phenomenon down to a very simple level, focusing on minimal groups and performance of a simple experimental task. Discrimination is measured simply in terms of how much money these boys allocated to each other.

About ethnocentrism?

It is clearly an issue that is relevant to this study as Tajfel's aim was to examine group behaviour and in particular, behaviour towards out-groups. The participants were clearly seen to favour their own group perhaps because of the ethnocentric belief that their group was superior to all others.

IS THE STUDY USEFUL?

The study deals with a destructive and anti-social, but very common feature of society, in examining the causes of prejudice and discrimination. As such, it can be seen as a very useful piece of research that could be used to improve everyday life. However, the applications are restricted by the methodological limitations such as low ecological validity, an unrepresentative sample and the reductionist principles adopted.

HOT EXAM HINT

You should be able to:
- describe the aim, sample, method, results and conclusions of the study
- describe the strengths and weaknesses of laboratory experiments.

FOR CONSIDERATION

1 How do you think the results of this study would change if other groups were tested such as females, adults, younger children, other cultural groups?
2 Suggest a different method of examining prejudice and discrimination that would have higher ecological validity.
3 Based on the results of this study, how do you think prejudice can be reduced?
4 How could prejudice and discrimination be studied in real life?

USEFUL RESOURCES

HOT EXAM HINTS

STRENGTHS OF THE SOCIAL APPROACH INCLUDE THE FOLLOWING:

- Demonstrating the extent to which situational factors affect human behaviour (Milgram).
- Collecting a scope of quantitative and qualitative data.
- Field studies have high ecological validity.
- Investigates issues which are highly relevant to society (e.g. Tajfel).

WEAKNESSES OF THE SOCIAL APPROACH INCLUDE THE FOLLOWING:

- May be unethical.
- Laboratory studies lack ecological validity.
- Highly dependent on culture and social context.
- Results may not generalize to other groups of participants.
- Demand characteristics may be high.

CD-ROM

Revision: Crosswords: Social

BOOKS

Gross, R. (2001) *Psychology: The Science of Mind of Behaviour*, Hodder & Stoughton, 4th edn.
This is an excellent general psychology textbook and chapters 25, 26, 27 and 30 will give you plenty of information on the topics covered in this section.

Two easy-to-read texts covering a range of social psychology topics:
Aronson, Eliot (1976) *The Social Animal*, Freeman.
Cialdini, Robert (1993) *Influence: Science and Practice*, HarperCollins.

Milgram, Stanley (1974) *Obedience to Authority*, Pinter and Martin.
A truly fascinating account of Milgram's research in his own words. Contains an excellent section justifying the research and explaining the debrief and follow-up procedures.

WEBSITES

www.heinemann.co.uk/hotlinks and insert the code 670XP.
Look at the websites listed under Social: Useful websites.

CHAPTER 6

THE INDIVIDUAL DIFFERENCES APPROACH

THE CORE STUDIES

WHAT IS THE PSYCHOLOGY OF INDIVIDUAL DIFFERENCES?

The individual differences approach is more difficult to describe than the approaches we have looked at previously. In general terms, this approach looks at the differences *between* people, whereas previous approaches have tended to look at factors that are common to all people. This approach covers intelligence and personality and the way that these have been tested, concepts and definitions of normality and abnormality, and a huge range of descriptions and explanations of a variety of mental health disorders.

THE CORE STUDIES

Gould (1982)

This is a **review article** that highlights some major problems in the history and development of intelligence tests. It concentrates on mass testing conducted during the First World War with US army recruits.

Hraba and Grant (1970)

This is a **replication** of an earlier study conducted by Clark and Clark in 1939. They had discovered that black American children would choose a black doll rather than a white doll when asked questions such as 'Which doll is a nice doll?'. Hraba and Grant's results suggest that the social and political changes that had taken place between the two studies had led the black children to have a more positive attitude towards their own race.

Rosenhan (1973)

This is a study using the technique of **participant observation**. Several people including Rosenhan himself 'faked' the symptoms of schizophrenia in order to gain admission to psychiatric wards. The results suggest that labelling patients as mentally ill makes it very hard for hospital staff to recognise that they are, in fact, sane.

Thigpen and Cleckley (1954)

This is a fascinating **case study** of a woman with multiple personality disorder. This is a controversial diagnosis and many people would argue that it does not exist. In the study, the authors present a range of data in support of their claim that this was a genuine case.

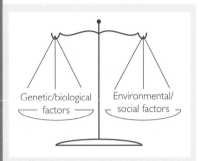

Fig. 6.1 *The nature-nurture debate*

 KEY DEFINITIONS

INTELLIGENCE
Goal-directed, adaptive behaviour.
(Sternberg, 1995)

Judgement, practical sense, initiative, the faculty of adapting one's self to circumstances. To judge well, to comprehend well, to reason well, these are the essential activities of intelligence.
(Binet and Simon, 1916)

WHAT IS THE NATURE-NURTURE DEBATE?

The nature-nurture debate considers the role of **genetic/biological** factors versus **environmental/social** factors in determining a range of behaviours. One of the most controversial nature-nurture debates concerns **intelligence**. On one side is the argument that differences in intelligence are largely determined by genetic factors and opposing this is the argument that differences in intelligence can be explained in terms of environmental factors.

WHAT IS INTELLIGENCE?

Intelligence is a remarkably difficult concept to define. We all know what we mean when we say that someone is intelligent, but it is very difficult to *explain* what we mean by this. The Collins English Dictionary defines intelligence simply as 'the capacity for understanding' and 'the ability to perceive and comprehend meaning' and it is interesting how many psychology texts do not even try to give a definition. Sternberg (1995) points out that there are probably as many definitions of intelligence as there are intelligence researchers!

HOW HAS INTELLIGENCE BEEN TESTED?

Intelligence tests were first devised by Binet in 1905 and were designed to identify children in need of remedial education. This carries with it the assumption that intelligence could change, but as we will see this notion was discarded by later researchers. Binet devised a test of 'general mental ability' including both verbal and non-verbal tasks. The scores were based on a comparison with the performance of the 'average' child at each age and gave a result called an **intelligence quotient (IQ)** which is still used today.

IQ for children is calculated by establishing the child's mental age (MA) and dividing this by their chronological or actual age (CA) and then multiplying by 100:

- A child with a CA of 8 and an MA of 10 will have an IQ of 120 (10/8 × 100).
- A child with a CA of 10 and an MA of 8 will have an IQ of 80 (8/10 × 100).
- A child with a CA of 10 and an MA of 10 will have an IQ of 100 (10/10 × 100).

Binet's aim had been to identify children who were not achieving as much as others of the same age, in order that they could be helped to improve. This assumes that intelligence is not a fixed quantity but that it could change. However, IQ tests were used in very different ways by other people.

Goddard took Binet's tests to America and suggested that they could be used to recognise people's innate abilities so that they could be segregated (set apart). Goddard was a strong supporter of the genetic basis of intelligence and was a **eugenicist**.

Goddard also added to the categories of mental deficiency that were in current use. 'Idiots' were those adults with mental ages of below 3 and 'imbeciles' were adults with mental ages of between 3 and 7. Goddard added the category of 'moron' (from the Greek word moros meaning foolish) to describe what he called 'high grade defectives', whose mental ages were between 8 and 12 (IQ of between 50 and 70). This is where the title of the core study by Gould ('A nation of morons') comes from.

WHAT PROBLEMS ARE THERE WITH INTELLIGENCE TESTS?

This is not the place to explore fully all the issues surrounding intelligence tests. However, it is important that you understand that while intelligence tests have altered significantly since their first use around 100 years ago, they are not without their problems today. Some of the key issues are discussed below.

Cultural bias

IQ tests measure success according to the criteria of a particular culture. Other cultures may have very different notions of 'intelligence'.

There have been many attempts to produce culture free or culture fair tests. This has proved to be very difficult, which in itself suggests that intelligence has a cultural (or environmental) basis.

Motivation

People will do better on tests if they understand their purpose and have some motivation for doing them. For example, Brazilian children who worked as street vendors were able to demonstrate complex arithmetical skills when selling things, but were not able to do this in test situations.

Familiarity with test materials/testing

IQ scores improve if the person has some experience of taking tests. The type of questions asked in IQ tests are fairly familiar to people in some countries but would be a very strange experience to people from some other countries.

The core study described in the next section is a **review** of one of the early mass intelligence tests. The tests were conducted by Robert M Yerkes during the First World War using US army recruits. In the review Gould is highly critical of the methods used by Yerkes and the uses to which his data were put.

GOULD (1982): THE CORE STUDY

WHAT WAS THE AIM OF THE REVIEW?

The aim of the review was to give a **critical account** of one episode in the history of IQ testing.

In 1915, mental testing was a new field. Unfortunately, it was practised by people who had not been properly trained in the administration of the tests, leading to absurd results. Robert M Yerkes agreed with critics that the tests and the testing procedures could be improved but felt that this was an opportunity to establish psychology as a rigorous scientific discipline.

WHO DID YERKES TEST?

At the start of the First World War, Yerkes won agreement from the US government to allow him to administer IQ tests to 1.75 million army recruits. Working with Terman and Goddard and other colleagues, he designed specific tests to use with the recruits.

They designed three types of tests. The **Army Alpha** test was written for those recruits who could read and write. For those recruits who could not read and write (and for those who had failed the Alpha test), a pictorial test called the **Army Beta** was designed. If they failed this test, they would be recalled for an **individual spoken test.**

WHAT DID THE TESTS SHOW?

The results discussed by Gould were produced by Boring who conducted a statistical analysis of 160,000 cases. Three 'facts' emerged from the data:
- The average mental age of white American males was 13. This is just above the level of 'moronity'.
- European immigrants could be graded by their country of origin. The average man of many nations was a moron, but the darker people of southern Europe and the Slavs of eastern Europe were less intelligent than the fair people of western and northern Europe.
- Black people had the lowest mental age at just 10.41.

WHAT WERE THE EFFECTS OF THESE RESULTS?

The most profound effect of the publication of these results was their impact on the immigration debate. This was a major political debate at the time and Gould acknowledges that there may well have been restrictions on immigration without the publication of these data. However, he asserts that the data had a major impact on the way in which restrictions were set. The 1924 Immigration Restriction Act reset immigration quotas in such a way that southern and eastern Europeans were effectively barred. Estimates suggest that up to six million people

What do you think the following
questions are measuring?

- Crisco is a: *patent medicine,
  disinfectant, toothpaste, food product*

- Christy Mathewson is famous as a:
  writer, artist, baseball player, comedian

*Fig. 6.2 Example question
from the Beta test*

*Fig. 6.3 Example question
from the Beta test*

from these areas of Europe were denied access to the USA over the next 20 years. As Gould poignantly concludes in his article, 'We know what happened to many who wished to leave but had nowhere to go'.

WHAT PROBLEMS WERE THERE WITH THE TESTS?

The Alpha test contained some items that are similar to those found in modern intelligence tests (identify the next number in a sequence, analogies, anagrams). However, some items are described by Gould as 'ludicrous', particularly given that the tests were claiming to measure **native intellectual ability**, that is, intelligence unaffected by environment or experience.

The Beta test contained pictures with missing parts and tasks where the soldier had to find the next number in a series or translate a series of symbols into numbers. These tests were still measuring cultural knowledge and some even required knowledge of numbers and written answers!

WHAT ARE THE STUDY'S CONCLUSIONS?

Gould argues convincingly that the tests were not an accurate reflection of people's intelligence but a reflection of their knowledge of US culture and their basic literacy skills.

WHAT PROBLEMS WERE THERE WITH THE ADMINISTRATION OF THE TESTS?

Gould identifies several problems with the ways the tests were administered:
- Recruits were allocated to Alpha and Beta tests differently in different camps. In some camps, schooling to third grade level was required to take the Alpha test, in another camp anyone who said he could read took the Alpha test.
- Recruits had spent less time in school than Yerkes had anticipated and the queues for the Beta test got longer and longer. This resulted in many recruits being wrongly allocated to the Alpha test even though they could not read and write.
- Recruits who had failed the Alpha test were rarely recalled for the Beta test.

The administration of the tests produced a situation in which new immigrants and black people in particular were systematically disadvantaged.

This is a disturbing episode in the history of psychology. It is difficult to look at this now without thinking that the problems must have been obvious. It shows clearly how beliefs can triumph over reason and Gould concludes in his book that the eugenicists 'won one of the greatest victories of scientific racism in American history' (Gould, 1981).

THINKING LIKE A PSYCHOLOGIST – EVALUATING THE CORE STUDY

WHAT ARE THE STRENGTHS AND WEAKNESSES OF GOULD'S METHOD?

Review articles are slightly different from other methods used in psychological research. The author of a review does not collect data but comments on research conducted by another researcher. Gould's review offers a fresh perspective on what may be regarded as a highly regrettable episode in the history of psychology.

He highlights many problems both with the **collection** and **interpretation** of the data and, with the benefit of hindsight, is able to show how the conclusions drawn from Yerkes' work had major social and political consequences.

The review also highlights some of the strengths and weaknesses of the use of **psychometric tests** more generally. There is no doubt that many psychometric tests are valuable tools and allow for the testing and comparisons of large numbers of people relatively quickly and cheaply. If the tests are reliable and valid (see below), then they will be more objective than an individual opinion as to the personality characteristics or intelligence of a job applicant, for example. However, there are also many problems associated with the way tests are administered and scored and results should be treated with caution.

WAS THE SAMPLE REPRESENTATIVE?

This is a difficult question to answer. The sample of men tested by Yerkes totalled over 1.75 million army recruits. This has to be the largest sample of participants ever used in psychological research! However, the fact that there are so many questions over the way the tests were administered and the content of the tests makes it very unwise to generalise Yerkes' conclusions on intelligence to any other groups.

WHAT TYPE OF DATA WAS COLLECTED?

The data were **quantitative**. All Yerkes collected were the IQ scores as measured by his tests. Gould, however, does offer us some descriptions of the testing conditions which could be described as **qualitative** data and these descriptions add considerably to our understanding of the problems in Yerkes' research.

CD-ROM

The Individual Differences Approach: Web investigation: Gould

QUOTE

'It was touching to see the intense effort ... put into answering the questions, often by men who never before had held a pencil in their hands.' A Beta test examiner, cited in Gould

'In June it was found impossible to recall a thousand men listed for individual examination. In July Alpha failures among [black people] were not recalled.' Chief tester at Camp Dix, cited in Gould.

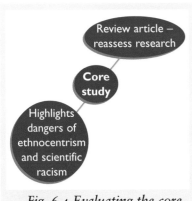

Fig. 6.4 *Evaluating the core study*

WHAT DOES THE STUDY TELL US ...

About the reliability and validity of intelligence tests?

Gould argues convincingly that the tests used by Yerkes were *neither reliable nor valid*. They were unreliable due to the many different ways in which people were tested and the fact that so many were given the wrong tests. They were not valid because they did not test native intellectual ability but cultural knowledge which could not possibly have been acquired by people who had only recently arrived in the country.

About ethnocentrism?

The review highlights the dangers of ethnocentrism. Yerkes and his colleagues were apparently 'blind' to the flaws in their research and their reasoning. These flaws look very obvious to us nearly a century later, but as we will see in the introduction to the core study by Hraba and Grant, American society was a very different place 100 years ago. The **unchallenged ethnocentric attitudes** of the researchers contribute to **'scientific racism'** where unsubstantiated arguments are presented as scientific and have damaging effects on particular groups of people. This is discussed further below.

About the nature-nurture debate?

People supporting a **eugenicist argument** would no doubt quote research like Yerkes' as support for their points of views. However, Gould's review shows clearly that whatever Yerkes was measuring was the result of **nurture** rather than nature. People scored highly on the tests if they spoke fluent English and were familiar with American culture. If not, they scored badly. This cannot be taken to support any argument that proposes the intellectual superiority of white people over black people as the tests were biased in favour of the white American recruits.

About social control?

The study highlights the dangers of scientific racism. Major political consequences resulted from the work conducted by Yerkes and huge numbers of lives were no doubt lost as a result of the Immigration Act. This illustrates the power of research and the dangers of taking such research at face value.

IS THE STUDY USEFUL?

Gould's review is very useful. It is important that people continue to question and reassess research that has taken place in the past. It also shows the importance of considering original research rather than simply accepting the brief summaries of results of studies that are often found in textbooks. It shows us the importance of being critical and always looking for details of how research was conducted.

HOT EXAM HINT

You should be able to:
- explain the research conducted by Yerkes and the major problems identified by Gould
- describe the strengths and weaknesses of reviews.

FOR CONSIDERATION

1 Is intelligence testing reductionist? Is intelligence more than can be measured by a pen and paper test?

2 Design a question that tests native intellectual ability. Does it involve pictures? If so, have a look again at the review by Deregowski (see page 22)!

3 Should researchers consider the ethical implications of their findings before publishing or is this a different form of social control?

HRABA AND GRANT (1970): BACKGROUND

ARE CHILDREN AWARE OF THEIR OWN RACE?

In the 1930s Horowitz conducted one of the first studies of children's awareness of their own race. She used picture techniques with 24 black and white children from 2 to 5 years of age. In the test, children were shown a pair of photographs showing a white child and a black child (these photographs were of either boys or girls depending on the child being tested), a pair of line drawings showing a white boy and a black boy and a set of line drawings depicting a white boy, a black boy, a clown and a chicken.

Boys were asked in each case to identify themselves. The form of the question was 'Show me which one is you. Which one is (using name of the subject)?'. The girls, after having identified themselves in the first item, were asked to identify brothers or cousins from the other sets of pictures.

Fig. 6.5 Horowitz's study involved showing white and black children a series of drawings

Horowitz found that around a third of children made incorrect identifications of their own race, although this did decrease with age. Clark and Clark replicated this study in 1939 and found similar results.

However, these studies only tell us about children's ability to identify their own race. They do not reveal anything about the children's feelings about their own or other races. Clark and Clark then conducted a similar study using dolls rather than pictures and photographs and asking about more than just racial self-identification. Clark and Clark asked questions designed to explore children's racial preference, their racial awareness or knowledge and finally their racial self-identification. They only tested black children in this study.

KEY CONCEPT

Kenneth and Mamie Clark were among the first African-American psychologists.

KEY CONCEPT

Questions measuring racial preference:

1 Give me the doll that you want to play with.
2 Give me the doll that is a nice doll.
3 Give me the doll that looks bad.
4 Give me the doll that is a nice colour.

Questions measuring racial awareness:

5 Give me the doll that looks like a white child.
6 Give me the doll that looks like a coloured child.
7 Give me the doll that looks like a Negro* child.
* The question used this now-discredited and inappropriate term.

Question measuring racial self-identification:

8 Give me the doll that looks like you.

Clark and Clark (1939)

WHAT DID CLARK AND CLARK FIND?

Racial preference

Clark and Clark found that the majority of the black children they tested preferred the white doll. For example, 67 per cent of the children wanted to play with the white doll and 59 per cent thought that the black doll 'looked bad'.

Racial awareness

Clark and Clark found that the majority of children could identify correctly the race of the doll.

Racial self-identification

Although most children identified themselves correctly, black children with light skin colour were far more likely to misidentify themselves.

These results suggest that at the time of the research, many black children had negative attitudes about their own race.

Fig. 6.6 Martin Luther King, civil rights campaigner, at the March on Washington

☕ FOR CONSIDERATION

In 1979, Hraba and Grant replicated the racial preference study conducted by Clark and Clark. Given all the changes in racial awareness in the four decades since the Clark and Clark study had been conducted, what would their results show?

WHERE MIGHT THESE NEGATIVE ATTITUDES HAVE COME FROM?

The US in 1939 was a very different place than today. It is only around 40 years ago that American society was heavily segregated. Black people had to drink at different drinking fountains from white people, they were only allowed to sit at the back of buses and there were 'white only' sections in cinemas.

Here are some of the changes that have taken place since 1939:

- **1954** US Supreme Court banned segregation in publicly funded schools.
- **1955** Bus boycott launched in Montgomery, Alabama after an African-American woman, Rosa Parks was arrested for refusing to give up her seat to a white person.
- **1956** After a year of boycotts, the Montgomery buses desegregated.
- **1957** At a previously all-white school in Little Rock, Arkansas, 1000 paratroopers were sent in by President Eisenhower to restore order and escort nine black students to their classes.
- **1961** Freedom rides began from Washington DC as groups of black and white people travelled on buses through the still segregated southern states to challenge segregation.
- **1962** Two people were killed and many injured in riots over the admission of the first black student, James Meredith, to the University of Mississippi.
- **1963** The Reverend Martin Luther King and other ministers demonstrating in Birmingham, Alabama, were arrested. Police used dogs and fire hoses to 'control' the peaceful protest.
- **1963** 250,000 people attended the March on Washington, urging support for pending civil rights legislation. This was the demonstration at which Martin Luther King made his famous 'I have a dream' speech.
- **1963** Four girls were killed in the bombing of a Baptist church in Birmingham, Alabama, by members of the Ku Klux Klan.
- **1964** Three civil rights workers were murdered in Mississippi.
- **1964** President Johnson signed the Civil Rights Act.
- **1965** Malcolm X was murdered.
- **1965** President Johnson signed the Voting Rights Act. The Act suspended devices such as literacy tests that aimed to prevent African-Americans from voting.
- **1965** Riots left 34 people dead in Los Angeles.
- **1968** Martin Luther King was assassinated in Memphis, Tennessee. His murder unleashed violence in over 100 American cities.
- **1978** The US Supreme Court outlawed racial quotas in a lawsuit brought by a white man who had been turned down by the medical school at the University of California.
- **1989** Douglas Wilder of Virginia became America's first African-American state Governor.
- **1992** Race riots erupted in Los Angeles and other cities after a jury acquitted police officers of the (videotaped) beating of Rodney King, an African-American.

HRABA AND GRANT (1970): THE CORE STUDY

WHAT WAS THE AIM OF THE STUDY?

The study examined the racial preferences of both black and white children in an inter-racial setting.

HOW WAS THE RESEARCH CARRIED OUT?

This study replicated the method used by Clark and Clark (1939) as closely as possible. Each child was interviewed using a set of four dolls, two black and two white. They were asked the same questions as had been used in the study by Clark and Clark (see page 134).

Children were also asked to name and indicate the race of their best friends and their teachers were also asked for this information. This was to try and measure the behavioural consequence of racial preference and identification.

FOR CONSIDERATION

How do you think the results might differ from Clark and Clark's original study?

WHO WERE THE PARTICIPANTS?

The 160 children, aged 4–8 years old, all came from five public schools in Lincoln, Nebraska. They included 89 black children and 71 white children drawn at random from the same classes.

WHAT WERE THE RESULTS?

Racial preference

'Give me the doll that you want to play with'

	Black doll	**White doll**	**Don't know/ no response**
Black children (1939)	32%	67%	
Black children (1969)	70%	30%	
White children (1969)	16%	83%	1%

'Give me the doll that is a nice doll'

	Black doll	**White doll**	**Don't know/ no response**
Black children (1939)	38%	59%	3%
Black children (1969)	54%	46%	
White children (1969)	30%	70%	

Fig. 6.7 'Give me the doll that you want to play with'

Racial awareness (or knowledge)

'Give me the doll that looks like a white child'

	Correct responses
Black children (1939)	94%
Black children (1969)	90%

'Give me the doll that looks like a coloured child'

	Correct responses
Black children (1939)	93%
Black children (1969)	93%

'Give me the doll that looks like a black (Negro) child'

	Correct responses
Black children (1939)	72%
Black children (1969)	86%

The results are only given for black children. As you can see from the tables, there is little difference between 1939 and 1969 in response to questions 5 and 6, and a higher proportion of children correctly identified the 'Negro' doll in 1969.

Fig. 6.8 Which dolls might these children choose?

'Give me the doll that looks bad'

	Black doll	White doll	Don't know/ no response
Black children (1939)	59%	17%	
Black children (1969)	36%	61%	3%
White children (1969)	63%	34%	3%

'Give me the doll that is a nice colour'

	Black doll	White doll	Don't know/ no response
Black children (1939)	38%	60%	2%
Black children (1969)	69%	31%	
White children (1969)	49%	48%	3%

We can see that black children have a **more positive sense of their own race** than those tested by Clark and Clark 40 years earlier. There are still signs of **negative feelings** though as demonstrated by the fact that nearly half of the black children chose the white doll as the 'nice doll'.

'Give me the doll that looks like you' – Only 15 per cent of black children with light skin colour in the 1969 study chose the white doll in response to this question.

The race of the interviewer appeared to have no significant effect on the children's responses to any of the questions. There was also no relationship between doll choice and friendship choice.

WHAT ARE THE STUDY'S CONCLUSIONS?

The social changes that took place in the USA between the original study and this replication may be responsible for the changes in racial preference demonstrated by the children. Increased inter-racial contact (due to desegregation) and more black role models will also have affected the racial awareness and racial preferences of the children.

THINKING LIKE A PSYCHOLOGIST – EVALUATING THE CORE STUDY

WHAT ARE THE STRENGTHS AND WEAKNESSES OF HRABA AND GRANT'S METHOD?

The method is **quasi-experimental** as the researchers did not have control over the independent variable (the race of the children). Quasi-experimental designs are suitable for research where the independent variable varies naturally and cannot be manipulated by the experimenter. The research was also a replication of a previous study. Replications are useful in confirming previous findings or in highlighting differences between the original study and the replication. In this case, the replication suggests the massive social changes that had taken place between 1939 and 1969 are responsible for the differences in the way the children responded to the questions. It is now more than 30 years since Hraba and Grant conducted this study and it is possible that a further replication would reveal more differences in racial preferences.

WAS THE SAMPLE REPRESENTATIVE?

Hraba and Grant tested a large sample of children drawn from five different schools in Lincoln, Nebraska. Eighty-nine of the children were black and these children represented 60 per cent of the black children in the age group studied in these schools. This would suggest that Hraba and Grant had a representative sample of black children aged between 4 and 8 years in public school in Lincoln, Nebraska. Whether it can be assumed that these children are representative of black children in other parts of the USA is not so clear. It could be argued that differences between the area where the children lived in the original study and Lincoln may be large enough to account for the differences found. Children living in areas where there are far bigger black populations may also have very different attitudes to their own race. Lastly, the research has focused on simple distinctions between black and white people and this does not in any way represent the vast diversity of race.

WHAT TYPE OF DATA WAS COLLECTED?

The data were **quantitative**. We simply know how many children chose the black doll and the white doll in response to each question. It would have been interesting to know a little more in relation to these questions. For example, why did children choose a particular doll, what made them think that the doll looked bad, or nice, or what exactly about the doll did they think looked like them? Did they have a strong preference for one doll or were they just picking one because they had been asked to?

FOR CONSIDERATION

Design a study testing racial preference and collecting qualitative data. What strengths and weaknesses do you think your study has?

KEY CONCEPT

The core study by Samuel and Bryant would support the notion that children might feel that they had to choose a different doll every time they were asked a question (see page 44).

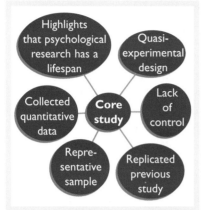

Fig. 6.9 Evaluating the core study

HOT EXAM HINT

You should be able to:
- describe the aim, sample, method, results and conclusion of this study (it is not necessary for you to learn numerical results so long as you can describe them in words)
- describe the strengths and weaknesses of quasi-experimental designs and of replications.

FOR CONSIDERATION

1 Think about the concept of reinforcement. How could reinforcement explain the learning of prejudiced attitudes and behaviours?
2 How could prejudice be reduced?
3 How else could you measure children's racial preferences?
4 Suggest two improvements that could be made to Hraba and Grant's procedure.
5 Which other core studies may be 'out of date'? Which ones would be interesting to replicate in the twenty-first century?

CAN THE STUDY BE APPLIED TO REAL LIFE?

The study attempted to measure racial preference and racial awareness by using dolls. It could be argued that doll choice does not necessarily tell us anything about the child's attitudes to their own race. Hraba and Grant point out that there was no relationship between doll preference and choice of best friends for either the black or the white children. We are not given details about the dolls except that four were used, two black and two white and 'identical in all other respects'. How were they dressed? Were they meant to be male or female? The collection of qualitative data might have revealed more about each child's reason for picking a particular doll. There may also have been some demand characteristics in the procedure of the study. Children were asked eight questions and they may have made the assumption that they needed to choose a different doll in response to each of the questions.

WHAT DOES THE STUDY TELL US ABOUT ETHNOCENTRISM?

The study shows us that both white and black children were ethnocentric in the sense that they were more likely to choose a doll of their own race as the 'nice doll' and a doll of the other race as the 'bad doll'. In fact, the study perhaps reveals more about the white children's ethnocentric attitudes than the black children's racial preferences. The study also strongly suggests that these attitudes are social in nature and will change in response to social changes.

IS THE RESEARCH USEFUL?

The study highlights a number of useful points. First, it demonstrates the fact that the results of psychological research have a **'lifespan'**. Findings from the 1930s may not have anything useful to tell us about behaviours today. This suggests that we should be aware of the **social and political context**, as well as the culture, in which a piece of research is conducted. Second, the research suggests that racial preferences are learned and this might lead to suggestions about how negative attitudes could be 'unlearned'.

SECTION **7** | # ROSENHAN (1973): BACKGROUND

CAN ABNORMALITY BE DEFINED?

The core study by Rosenhan which will be considered in the next section suggests that *it is not possible objectively to define abnormality*. There are several reasons why this might be the case. Abnormality cannot be defined statistically. It may seem logical to suggest that what is considered abnormal will also be unusual or statistically rare. This may be true of some behaviours that we consider to be abnormal, but there are many other behaviours which might be considered abnormal which are in fact statistically quite common. For example, the incidence of depression in the general population is high enough to be considered statistically common.

In addition to this, many **desirable behaviours** such as very high intelligence or musical or artistic talent are infrequent enough to be considered 'abnormal', but we would not label them in quite the same way. This suggests that abnormality is **defined socially or culturally** and this is confirmed by the points made below:

Definitions of abnormality are not universal

What is considered abnormal in one culture may not be considered abnormal in another culture. Hearing voices is considered a classic sign of schizophrenia in our culture but may be viewed very differently in another culture. Paranoid behaviour (for example assuming that everyone is likely to take advantage of us) is considered 'abnormal' in this culture, but Mead (1935) described this pattern of behaviour as the norm among the Mundugumor people, even between male members of the same household. Malinowski (1929) described as the norm the wearing of a dead husband's or father's jawbones as a necklace. There is no doubt that in our culture, we would regard this behaviour as highly abnormal.

Definitions of abnormality are not stable

As well as cultural differences in the definitions of abnormality, definitions change over time. Probably the best example of this relates to homosexuality, which was still classified in the American Psychiatric Association's official classification system (DSM) in 1968. In 1973, this was changed to 'sexual orientation disturbance' which describes only gay men and women who are disturbed by, and wish to change their sexual orientation, and later still to 'ego-dystonic homosexuality', a term defined as someone who is homosexually aroused and finds this arousal distressing. DSM does recognise that this is likely to be the result of social attitudes but as Gross (2001) notes, this means that according to DSM 'a homosexual is abnormal if s/he has been persuaded by society's prejudices that homosexuality is inherently abnormal, but at the same time it denied that homosexuality in itself is abnormal'.

FOR CONSIDERATION

What do you think abnormal means? What do you think normal means?

KEY CONCEPT

Recent figures from the mental health charity MIND suggest that one person in every four will suffer from some form of mental illness at some point in their life.

KEY CONCEPT

There is an acute anxiety/panic disorder reported in south-east Asia, south China and India called Koro, in which male sufferers believe that their penis will suddenly withdraw into their abdomen or in females, that the breasts, labia or vulva will retract into their body. There is nothing like this disorder described in western psychiatry. (Finerman, 1994; cited in Gross, 2001)

CD-ROM

The Individual Differences Approach: Culture-bound syndrome, and Historical treatments for mental illness

Fig. 6.10 Can abnormality be defined?

KEY CONCEPT

Some of the disorders included in the current version of ICD-10:

Schizophrenic and other psychotic disorders
Substance related disorders
Mood disorders
Anxiety disorders
Personality disorders
Sexual and gender identity disorders
Sleep disorders
Eating disorders

KEY DEFINITIONS

RELIABILITY
Consistency. The diagnostic criteria should ensure that the same diagnosis will be made regardless of who is doing the diagnosing.

VALIDITY
Correctness. The diagnostic criteria should ensure that genuine disorders are being diagnosed accurately.

There are many other examples of cultural and historical shifts in the definitions of abnormality which allow us to conclude that there is no objectively determined 'normal and abnormal'. Rather such judgements are **social ones** and can therefore be different depending on who is doing the judging.

HOW IS PSYCHIATRIC DIAGNOSIS MADE?

Psychiatry uses **classification systems** to identify and diagnose mental health disorders. The World Health Organisation developed a manual of all diseases and disorders, including those that are considered to be primarily psychological in nature. This manual is known as the International Standard Classification of Diseases, Injuries and Causes of Death (ICD). A similar system (DSM) is in use in America, and other countries such as China have their own classification systems.

For each disorder, there is a specified list of symptoms which must be present for a specified period of time for that diagnosis to be made. Diagnosis is also made on the basis of information about age and gender, other disorders which might be present and the personal and social consequences of the disorder.

Classifications should be both **reliable** and **valid**. Rosenhan's famous study investigates these issues in relation to the classification of schizophrenia by psychiatrists working in US hospitals. Are psychiatrists able to tell the difference between those who are genuinely mentally ill and those who are not? Once someone has been diagnosed as schizophrenic, is it possible to judge their behaviour without the effects of this label?

ROSENHAN (1973): THE CORE STUDY

WHAT WAS THE AIM OF THE STUDY?

The study posed the question: 'Can sanity and insanity be distinguished?'.

HOW WAS THE RESEARCH CARRIED OUT?

The first part of the study was a **field experiment** (with the independent variable being the behaviour of the pseudopatients) using **participant observation**. The second part of the study was **experimental**.

HOW WAS THE RESEARCH CARRIED OUT?

The pseudopatients made appointments at the hospital and claimed to have been hearing voices which were unclear but included words such as 'empty', 'hollow' and 'thud'. The voice was the same sex as the pseudopatient but was otherwise unfamiliar. The pseudopatients gave false names and occupations but reported every other aspect of the life history and personal circumstances correctly. Once they were admitted to the psychiatric ward, the pseudopatient stopped displaying any symptoms of abnormality. They behaved normally, spoke to people normally and responded appropriately to requests and instructions. If they were asked how they felt, they replied that they felt fine and were no longer experiencing symptoms.

WHAT WERE THE RESULTS OF THE FIRST STUDY?

The major finding was that the pseudopatients were not 'discovered'. The length of time the pseudopatients spent in hospital varied from seven to 52 days, with a mean of 19 days. This suggests that once they had been labelled as schizophrenic, it was virtually impossible for their behaviour to be interpreted in any other way.

Interestingly, several other patients did detect the pseudopatients. During the first three hospitalisations 35 of a total of 118 patients on the admissions ward made comments such as 'You're not sick, you're a professor checking up on the hospital'.

A perfectly normal report by a male pseudopatient of the relationships with his parents was translated within the **psychopathological context** into something very different. This shows how easily information can be distorted to fit the preconceived ideas held by the hospital staff.

The pseudopatients took notes. Initially, they did this in secret, but when it became clear that no one was bothered by this behaviour, they did so publicly. In the case of one pseudopatient, the comment 'patient engages in writing behaviour' was commonly used in nursing records.

REMEMBER

The participants were the hospital staff of the 12 hospitals. The **pseudopatients** (acting as if they were patients) were the **experimenters**. Three women and five men of varying ages and occupations acted as pseudopatients (some more than once).

KEY CONCEPT

Hearing voices is a classic symptom of schizophrenia. However, Rosenhan explains that they chose these particular words because they would suggest an existential crisis (my life is empty and meaningless) and because there are no specific published reports of existential psychosis.

FOR CONSIDERATION

Eleven were initially admitted with a diagnosis of schizophrenia (and the twelfth with a diagnosis of manic-depression). They were discharged with the diagnosis of schizophrenia 'in remission', in itself a rare diagnostic label.

The diagnosis 'schizophrenia in remission' is interesting because it means that the hospital staff had not detected that the pseudopatient was, in fact, sane but recognised simply that they were not displaying any symptoms at the present time.

FOR CONSIDERATION

The pseudopatient described a warm relationship with his mother but a more distant relationship with his father which improved during his adolescence. He described a good relationship with his wife and children, who he had rarely smacked. The case summary prepared by the psychiatrist described 'a long history of considerable ambivalence in close relationships ... Affective stability is absent ... punctuated by angry outbursts ...'.

Fig. 6.11 The pseudopatient engages in writing behaviour

 FOR CONSIDERATION

Patients queuing up early for lunch were described by a psychiatrist as exhibiting signs of oral-acquisitive syndrome, when the truth was probably that they were just bored and had nothing else to do!

 KEY CONCEPT

Rosenhan conducted a similar kind of study on a university campus and found that people were invariably helped (with the exception of one person who had been asking for directions to a psychiatrist's office).

HOW AS THE PSEUDOPATIENTS' BEHAVIOUR EXPLAINED?

The behaviour of the pseudopatients tended to be explained in terms of **individual characteristics** (primarily the fact that they were **schizophrenic**) rather than in terms of the situation in which they were observed. Pacing the corridor was interpreted as a sign of anxiety until the pseudopatient explained that he was just bored.

The pseudopatients also collected data on the way that hospital staff interacted with patients. As well as the data shown in the table, they reported that little eye contact was made with patients.

Hospital staff interaction with patients

Interaction	Response rates
Responses to requests made to psychiatrists	13 responses to a total of 185 requests = 7%
Responses to requests made to nurses and attendants	47 responses to a total of 1,283 requests = 3.6%
Amount of time spent with psychologists, psychiatrists, etc.	Average = less than 7 minutes a day

Finally, Rosenhan describes the effects of hospitalisation in terms of **powerlessness and depersonalisation**:

'... the patient is deprived of many of his legal rights ... his freedom of movement is restricted, he cannot initiate contact with staff... personal privacy is minimal, his personal history is available to any staff member (including volunteers) who chooses to read his file, and toilets may have no doors'.

WHAT HAPPENED IN THE SECOND STUDY?

A large teaching and research hospital heard about these findings and staff were doubtful that such a error could occur there. Rosenhan set up the following experiment.

He informed staff that sometime during the following three months, one or more pseudopatients would attempt to gain admission to the hospital. Each staff member was asked to rate each new patient on their likelihood of being a pseudopatient. Judgements were collected on 193 patients. Forty-one patients were alleged to be pseudopatients by at least one member of staff, 23 were judged as likely to be pseudopatients by at least one psychiatrist and 19 suspected by a psychiatrist and one other member of staff. There were, in fact, no pseudopatients. Of course, there is no way of knowing whether the 19 people judged as sane by two members of staff were actually sane or not, but as Rosenhan points out, 'Any diagnostic process that lends itself to massive errors of this sort cannot be a very reliable one'.

THINKING LIKE A PSYCHOLOGIST – EVALUATING THE CORE STUDY

WHAT ARE THE STRENGTHS AND WEAKNESSES OF ROSENHAN'S METHOD?

Field experiments have the major advantage of being conducted in a real environment and this gives the research **high ecological validity**. However, it is not possible to have as many controls in place as would be possible in a laboratory experiment. **Participant observation** allows the collection of highly detailed data without the problem of demand characteristics. As the hospitals did not know of the existence of the pseudopatients, there is no possibility that the staff could have changed their behaviour because they knew they were being observed. However this does raise serious **ethical issues** (see below) and there is also the possibility that the presence of the pseudopatient would change the environment they were observing.

WAS THE SAMPLE REPRESENTATIVE?

Strictly speaking, the sample is the 12 hospitals that were studied. Rosenhan ensured that this included a range of old and new institutions as well as those with different sources of funding. The results revealed little differences between the hospitals. This suggests that it is probably reasonable to generalise from this sample and suggest that the same results would be found in other hospitals.

WHAT TYPE OF DATA WAS COLLECTED?

There is a huge variety of data reported in this study, ranging from **quantitative** data detailing how many days each pseudopatient spent in the hospital and how many times pseudopatients were ignored by staff through to **qualitative** descriptions of the experiences of the pseudopatients. One of the strengths of this study could be seen as the wealth of data that are reported and there is no doubt that the conclusions reached by Rosenhan are well illustrated by the qualitative data that he has included.

IS THE STUDY ETHICAL?

Strictly speaking, the study is not ethical. The staff were deceived as they did not know that they were being observed and you need to consider how they might have felt when they discovered the research had taken place. Was the study justified? This is more difficult as there is certainly no other way that the study could have been conducted so you need to consider whether the results justified the deception. This is discussed below.

CD-ROM

The Individual Differences Approach: Rosenhan

FOR CONSIDERATION

Try to think of a way in which this study could have been conducted without breaking ethical guidelines.

Do you think the research was justified?

WHAT DOES THE STUDY TELL US ...

About individual and situational explanations of behaviour?

The study suggests that once the patients were labelled, the label stuck. Everything they did or said was interpreted as typical of a schizophrenic (or manic depressive) patient. This means that the situation that the pseudopatients were in had a powerful impact on the way that they were judged. The hospital staff were not able to perceive the pseudopatients in isolation from their label and the fact that they were in a psychiatric hospital. This raises serious doubts about the **reliability** and **validity** of psychiatric diagnosis.

About reinforcement and social control?

The implications from the study are that patients in psychiatric hospitals are 'conditioned' to behave in certain ways by the environments that they find themselves in. Their behaviour is shaped by the environment (nurses assume that signs of boredom are signs of anxiety, for example) and if the environment does not allow them to display 'normal' behaviour, it will be difficult for them to be seen as normal. Labelling is a powerful form of social control. Once a label has been applied to an individual, everything they do or say will be interpreted in the light of this label.

Rosenhan describes pseudopatients going to flush their medication down the toilet and finding pills already there. This would suggest that so long as the patients were not causing anyone any trouble, very little checks were made.

IS THE STUDY USEFUL?

The study was certainly useful in highlighting the ways in which hospital staff interact with patients. There are many suggestions for improved hospital care/staff training that could be made after reading this study. However, it is possible to question some of Rosenhan's conclusions. If you went to the doctor falsely complaining of severe pains in the region of your appendix and the doctor admitted you to hospital, you could hardly blame the doctor for making a faulty diagnosis. Isn't it better for psychiatrists to err on the side of caution and admit someone who is not really mentally ill than to send away someone who might be genuinely suffering? This does not fully excuse the length of time that some pseudopatients spent in hospital acting perfectly normally, but it does go some way to supporting the actions of those making the initial diagnosis.

Fig. 6.12 Evaluating the core study

HOT EXAM HINT

You should be able to:
- explain the aim, method, results and conclusions of both the studies reported by Rosenhan
- describe the strengths and weaknesses of field experiments and participant observation.

FOR CONSIDERATION

1 How would you feel if you were a member of staff working in one of these hospitals? How might you justify your behaviour?
2 What similarities can you identify between the effects of hospitalisation described in this study and the effects of imprisonment described in the study by Haney, Banks and Zimbardo (see page 106)?
3 What other labels are applied to people and what effects do these labels have?

THIGPEN AND CLECKLEY (1954): BACKGROUND

WHAT IS MULTIPLE PERSONALITY DISORDER?

Multiple Personality Disorder (MPD) is one of the most fascinating and controversial psychological conditions. It is not to be confused with schizophrenia as sufferers do not experience the emotional and cognitive disturbances typical of schizophrenia. Although the term schizophrenia means, literally, 'split-mind', this refers to the loss of unity between psychological functions.

In Multiple Personality Disorder, individually each of the personalities (alters) may be fully integrated and have distinct memories, behaviour patterns, social relationships and cognitive functioning. There is a long running debate over whether such a condition actually exists and when the core study by Thigpen and Cleckley was published (1954) there were virtually no cases in the literature.

Multiple Personality Disorder is now known as Dissociative Identity Disorder (DID) and this name reflects a growing professional understanding of the effects of severe trauma in childhood, most typically, extreme and repeated abuse.

WHAT IS DISSOCIATION?

Dissociation is described as a mental process which produces a **lack of connection** in a person's thoughts, memories, feelings, actions or sense of identity.

Some very mild forms of dissociation are familiar to us all, such as daydreaming, getting 'lost' in a book or film or driving on 'auto-pilot'. All of these experiences involve a lack of conscious awareness of your immediate surroundings. DID is at the extreme end of dissociative disorders (DD) and can result in profound problems. An extremely traumatic experience may result in the individual dissociating as a form of 'mental escape' from the fear and pain of the trauma. This is an extremely powerful defence against physical or emotional pain. If dissociation produces changes in memory, people who frequently dissociate may find their sense of personal history and identity are affected.

ARE THERE REALLY MULTIPLE PERSONALITIES?

MPD is now thought to be a somewhat misleading term. Although there are distinct 'entities' within a person, they are all manifestations of a single individual.

It is a highly controversial diagnosis and rates of MPD/DID have risen sharply in the US and are beginning to rise in the UK. Critics argue that

---

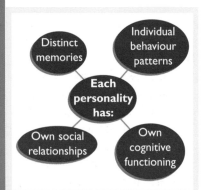

Fig. 6.13 The personalities in Dissociative Identity Disorder

Fig. 6.14 The Three Faces of Eve

this is due to the use of hypnosis and also that therapists are looking for multiples in people who are then subject to an extreme form of demand characteristics.

WHO WAS EVE?

Eve's real name was Christine Sizemore and she was first referred to a therapist at the age of 25 when she started suffering from severe and blinding headaches and occasional blackouts. Initially, the therapist felt that this was an 'ordinary case with commonplace symptoms' mostly surrounding marital difficulties. Eve White reported having no memory at all of a recent trip and this memory was recovered through the use of hypnosis.

A few days after the hypnosis, the therapist received an unsigned letter. The first part of this was Eve White's handwriting and was a coherent reflection of her recent therapy session. However, a paragraph had been added at the bottom of the letter in childlike handwriting. Eve denied having sent a letter although she agreed that she had started one and never finished it. She became extremely distressed on hearing about this letter and asked the therapist if hearing voices meant she was insane. She told the therapist that she had several times heard a clear voice addressing her. As the therapist wondered how to respond to this, Eve White put both hands to her head as if she were in pain. After a few moments her hand dropped and she said, in a bright voice, quite unlike her normal voice, 'Hi there Doc'.

Thigpen and Cleckley describe 'a thousand minute alterations of manner, gesture, expression, posture' which suggested to them that she was a completely different woman. Over the next 14 months and approximately 100 hours of interviewing, extensive material was gathered about Eve White's (and Eve Black's) life. It appeared as though Eve Black had had an independent existence since Eve White's childhood. When Eve Black is 'out' Eve White has no conscious awareness and was not even aware of the existence of Eve Black until informed by the therapist. Eve Black, however, maintains conscious awareness all of the time and describes the emotional, feelings and reactions of Eve White from an 'outsider's' point of view.

THIGPEN AND CLECKLEY (1954): THE CORE STUDY

WHAT WAS THE AIM OF THE STUDY?

The study is an extract from a longer book which includes much more detail about this case.

HOW WAS THE RESEARCH CARRIED OUT?

This is a **case study**. A huge amount of data were collected using EEG (electroencephalogram) recordings (of brain activity), psychometric and projective testing, and therapy sessions.

WHAT DID THE PSYCHOMETRIC AND PROJECTIVE TESTS REVEAL?

Both Eve White and Eve Black were given the following tests:
- the Wechsler-Bellevue Intelligence Scale
- Weschler Memory Scale
- drawings of human figures
- Rorschach (ink blot test).

The tests revealed Eve White to be serious, conscientious and anxious. In contrast, Eve Black was described as less anxious and more satisfied with superficial answers. Eve White scored 110 on the intelligence test and had the superior score on the memory test. Eve Black scored 104 on the intelligence test and achieved a fair score on the memory test. They both did badly on recall of digits.

The projective tests are more interesting. The dominant personality characteristic from interpretation of the projective tests was **repression** for Eve White and **regression** for Eve Black. The authors suggest that this regression symbolises a desire to return to an earlier stage of her life (possibly before her marriage, as Eve Black is actually the maiden name of Eve White). They suggest these tests do not reveal two distinct personalities but one personality at different stages of her life.

WHAT OTHER EVIDENCE IS THERE FOR MULTIPLE PERSONALITY?

The authors outline a number of events in Eve's life that suggest that she was suffering from multiple personality disorder. For example, Eve Black once bought several very expensive items of clothing and Eve White was unable to explain to her husband where they had come from. They also briefly mention a report from a distant relative who claimed that a previous marriage had taken place. Eve White denies any knowledge of this, but Eve Black finally admitted that this had been when she was in control for a significant length of time.

Fig. 6.15 *A variety of methods were used to collect data from Eve*

📖 QUOTE

"'When I go out and get drunk,' Eve Black with an easy wink once said to us, "she wakes up with the hangover".' (Thigpen and Cleckley, 1954)

✊ REMEMBER

The therapists describe Eve White and Eve Black as very different personalities. Eve White is described as quiet, feminine and dignified. Eve Black, on the other hand, is described as lacking compassion, shallow, hedonistic and irresponsible. She denies marriage to Eve White's husband and also denies any relationship to Eve White's daughter who she treats as an 'unconcerned bystander'.

💿 CD-ROM

The Individual Differences Approach: The Three Faces of Eve

WHAT HAPPENED NEXT?

After eight months of treatment, Eve White had made considerable progress. The headaches and blackouts had virtually gone and she had not heard voices since Eve Black revealed herself to the therapist. Eve Black, too, was causing 'less trouble', although she still 'got into bad company, picked up dates, and indulged in cheap and idle flirtations, her demure and conventional counterpart, lacking knowledge of these deeds, was spared the considerable humiliation and distress some of this conduct would otherwise have caused her' (Thigpen and Cleckley).

However, at this point in the therapy, things took a turn for the worse. The headaches returned and then the blackouts. More interestingly, Eve Black now experienced both the headaches and the blackouts, reporting to the therapist that 'I don't know where we go, but go we do'.

During one therapy session, Eve White appeared to fall asleep. After a few minutes, she opened her eyes and looked blankly around the room and said 'Who are you?'.

This was a third personality who called herself Jane. Jane is described by the authors as more mature, more vivid, more capable and more interesting than Eve White, and lacking the faults and inadequacies of Eve Black.

A little later, EEG readings were taken from all three personalities. The results showed some differences in the EEGs of the three personalities, with Eve Black being the most different (more signs of tension, restlessness and possible psychopathic tendencies, described as borderline normal). Eve White and Jane had more normal patterns and were difficult to distinguish from each other.

HOW DOES THE CORE STUDY END?

At the end of the article, the authors appear to be describing Jane as the 'solution'. They explain that she has awareness of both Eve White's and Eve Black's behaviour and thoughts although she does not have full access to their memories. She stays 'out' more and more although she can emerge only through Eve White. The authors point out that only superficially can she be regarded as a compromise between them.

THINKING LIKE A PSYCHOLOGIST – EVALUATING THE CORE STUDY

WHAT ARE THE STRENGTHS AND WEAKNESSES OF THIGPEN AND CLECKLEY'S METHOD?

This is a **case study**. This means that it is a detailed analysis of one individual. The depth of analysis and the richness of the data are a strength of case studies and there is no doubt that this study represents an enormous amount of research time.

The study also uses a range of psychometric and projective tests. Psychometric tests are simple to use and allow broad comparisons to be made and it is certainly interesting that Eve White and Eve Black show some distinct differences in their results. Projective tests are more subjective as they rely on the therapist's interpretation of the responses given by the patient and are therefore much more prone to bias and the effect of expectations. With both of these measures, it should be remembered that personality is not stable and any individual might achieve a different score if tested on several different occasions when in different moods.

WAS THE SAMPLE REPRESENTATIVE?

A case study is never representative of anyone other than the individual being studied. We can only really apply the results of this case study to helping the individual concerned. However, clinical case studies are very useful for other therapists, particularly when cases are highly unusual.

WHAT TYPE OF DATA WAS COLLECTED?

Both **qualitative** and **quantitative** data were collected and they complement each other. If only the scores from the intelligence and memory tests were available, the case that the authors are making for a diagnosis of multiple personality disorder would not be as convincing. If the article simply contained the descriptions of the differences (fascinating as they are), people might still be sceptical. Taken together, it can be argued that the authors present a strong case for the existence of more than one personality in Eve White.

WHAT DOES THE STUDY TELL US ABOUT THE NATURE-NURTURE DEBATE?

The study suggests that **environmental factors**, particularly traumatic events, can profoundly affect our mental health. While there may be convincing evidence that there is a **genetic predisposition** to certain mental health disorders, there is no doubt that they are triggered by

> ☕ **FOR CONSIDERATION**
>
> What other information could the therapists have collected? Are you convinced by their evidence?

Fig. 6.16 Evaluating the core study

HOT EXAM HINT

You should be able to:
- describe and evaluate the evidence that Thigpen and Cleckley offer in support of their diagnosis of MPD
- describe the strengths and weaknesses of case studies.

FOR CONSIDERATION

1 Think about the concept of reinforcement. Negative reinforcement is where unpleasant stimuli or experiences are avoided through particular behaviours. Is it possible to explain MPD in these terms?
2 Do you believe that Eve had three (or more) personalities? Are there any other explanations?
3 What is personality? Try to write a definition of personality. How many personalities have you got?

events in people's lives. In material published later than this study, information is given about a number of traumatic events that Eve had experienced. She had seen a man drown, and another man cut into pieces by a machine at a lumber mill, and had witnessed her mother very badly injured. There is little doubt that such events would have an effect on the mental health of a child even if you do not accept the diagnosis of MPD.

IS THE STUDY ETHICAL?

Does a therapist have the right to judge which personality is more deserving of survival than others? Some of the comments made about Eve Black are extremely judgemental and probably also sexist and dated. Therapists have a great deal of power over their patients and a responsibility to use this power wisely.

IS THE STUDY USEFUL?

Case studies are primarily useful in a **clinical** sense and this has been described above. This case study was the first fully documented case of multiple personality and it has no doubt led to the disorder being more easily recognised than at the time of this case. However, this is a highly controversial diagnosis and there is some concern that patients are being labelled incorrectly as suffering from this disorder.

Fig. 6.17 Therapists have a great deal of power over their patients and a responsibility to use this wisely

USEFUL RESOURCES

HOT EXAM HINTS

STRENGTHS OF THE INDIVIDUAL DIFFERENCES APPROACH INCLUDE THE FOLLOWING:

- The study of individual cases is invaluable in therapy.
- Psychometric tests allow comparisons to be drawn between people.
- This type of research highlights the influence of culture and experience (e.g. Gould, Hraba and Grant).

WEAKNESSES OF THE INDIVIDUAL DIFFERENCES APPROACH INCLUDE THE FOLLOWING:

- Psychometric tests have problems of reliability and validity.
- Case studies cannot be generalized.
- Some research ignored situational factors (e.g. Yerke's research described in Gould).
- May lead to social control.

CD-ROM

Revision: Crosswords: Individual differences

BOOKS

Gross, R. (2001) *Psychology: The Science of Mind of Behaviour*, Hodder & Stoughton, 4th edn.
This is an excellent general psychology textbook and chapters 33, 41, 43, 44 and 45 will give you plenty of information on the topics covered in this section.

Thigpen, C. and Cleckley, H. (1992) *The Three Faces of Eve*, Arcata Graphics.
This is the full account of the case study of Eve. It makes fascinating reading.

If you found the Three Faces of Eve fascinating, try these:
Schreiber, F. R. (1974) *Sybil*, Warner.
Keyes, D. (1995) *The Minds of Billy Milligan*, Penguin.

Prendergast, M. (1997) *Victims of Memory: Incest Accusations and Shattered Lives*. HarperCollins.
If you are more sceptical about the existence of MPD, you might find this interesting.

WEBSITES

Go to: www.heinemann.co.uk/hotlinks and insert the code 670XP.
Look at the websites listed under Individual Differences: Useful websites.

CHAPTER 7 PSYCHOLOGICAL INVESTIGATIONS

For this unit of the AS course, you have to conduct **four data collecting activities** as follows:

Activity A: Questions, self-reports and questionnaires.
Activity B: An observation.
Activity C: Comparison of data to investigate the difference between two conditions.
Activity D: A correlation.

These are not large research projects and you do not need to do a great deal of background research before you start. You should concentrate on the method (designing questions, observation schedules, and so on) and the results of each activity. Keep the activities simple and don't worry about collecting huge amounts of data. For most activities, ten participants will be plenty.

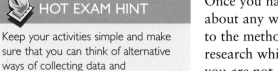

HOT EXAM HINT

Keep your activities simple and make sure that you can think of alternative ways of collecting data and improvements that could be made.

Once you have conducted your research, you should think carefully about any weaknesses and possible improvements that could be made to the method. Don't forget about ethics – you should not conduct any research which may be potentially distressing to your participants and you are not allowed to conduct experimental work with participants under the age of 16.

When you sit your examination, you are allowed to take your Practical Work Folder into the exam room with you. This is provided by OCR and will be given to you by your tutor in plenty of time. It will contain notes on the aim, method and results of your four data collecting activities. You will also be asked questions on information that is not in your folder and these questions will be of two types. You may be asked about:

- **general issues** relating to psychological research (strengths and weaknesses of methods, ethical issues, reliability and validity, and so on)
- **issues relating to the research that you have done** (weaknesses and how to overcome them, improvements, alternative methods of measuring variables, changes to sample/procedure and the effects of these).

It is therefore important that you spend *at least as much time considering these issues as you spend on the actual data collection.*

The following pages give you some guidance on how to conduct each activity, how to complete the Practical Work Folder and how to evaluate the work that you have done.

QUESTIONS, SELF-REPORTS AND QUESTIONNAIRES

Several of the core studies asked participants questions. For examples look at Loftus and Palmer (Chapter 2), Hodges and Tizard (Chapter 3), Schachter and Singer (Chapter 4), and Gould (Chapter 6).

Which other core studies asked people questions?

For this activity, you need to **question people directly** in some way. This could be a questionnaire on a suitable topic such as attitudes to sixth form or college, attitudes to issues such as healthy eating or recycling behaviour, study habits or sleep habits.

Your activity does not have to be a questionnaire. You could use **self-report** measures such as asking people how tired they are, how much they like a piece of music or even how much they enjoyed a particular core study! You could have **two conditions** for this activity and compare male and female responses to a question or series of questions or even conduct a piece of research into the effects of leading questions such as that conducted in the core study by Loftus and Palmer.

SOME ADVICE FOR CONDUCTING ACTIVITY A

- Don't ask too many questions – you don't want to be swamped with data! Even two or three questions may be enough depending on the topic, and you can always use the technique of 'distracter' questions and only analyse the key question(s).
- Keep participant numbers low. Ten participants would be enough for this activity.
- Don't spend too long getting the questions perfect. Think of it as a 'pilot' study – it will be much easier for you to evaluate.

DESIGNING YOUR QUESTIONS

There are many different ways to ask questions.

Why not 'pilot' your questionnaire on a couple of friends to make sure that the questions mean what you think they mean!

You can ask **open-ended** or **closed questions**. Open questions are simply questions to which the participant gives an answer. Closed questions give the participant a choice of answers to choose from. Closed questions are much easier to analyse, although a weakness would be that you are forcing participants to choose from the answers you have given and this might mean that the answer they give is not really a true reflection of their opinion. Open-ended questions allow people to say exactly what they want to but they are much harder to analyse.

If you are asking closed questions, think about how you would like people to answer. Below are several different examples of closed questions on the same topic:

Do you like being at college/in the sixth form? Yes/No

How much do you like being at college/in the sixth form?
I like it a lot
I quite like it

I don't like it much
I dislike it a lot

How much do you like being at college/in the sixth form?
1 2 3 4 5 6 7 8 9 10
Not at all   Very much

COMPLETING THE PRACTICAL WORK FOLDER

Keep this as simple as you can. Try to identify a few key questions and summarise the results. There is no need to do any statistical analysis on the data collected for this activity.

An example of a completed folder

HOT EXAM HINT

You are not allowed to include any evaluation of your activities in your folder, but you should consider possible strengths and weaknesses of what you have done. This is discussed in more detail on the next page.

ACTIVITY A: QUESTIONS, SELF-REPORTS AND QUESTIONNAIRES

<u>State the aim of this activity:</u>

The aim of this activity was to investigate attitudes to college.

<u>Give examples of the questions used, including any rating scales, etc.</u>

1 Do you like being at college? YES/NO
2 What AS subjects are you studying?
3 Rate your enjoyment of each subject on a 1–10 scale, where 1 = hate this subject and 10 = like this subject very much.
4 Do you think the amount of work you are set is:
   a far too much
   b a bit too much
   c about right
   d not enough

<u>Give details of the sample that you used for your investigation:</u>

20 students (10 male and 10 female)
Opportunity sample from common room
All aged 16–18 years

<u>Outline the procedure that you followed:</u>

Students were approached and asked if they could spare 5 minutes for a survey on attitudes to college life.

Those who agreed were given the questions on a piece of paper and sat in a quiet room to complete the questionnaire.

Participants were thanked/asked if they had any questions.

<u>Summarise your findings:</u>

1 16 people said they liked college and 4 said that they didn't.
2 The most common answers were English (11) and Biology (10).
3 The average rating was 6. The lowest rating was 1 (only one person/Sociology) and the highest was 10 (12 people gave one or more subject a score of 10).
4 The modal answer was b – a bit too much (12 people); 3 people said a – far too much; 5 said c – about right; and no one said d – not enough.

PREPARING FOR THE EXAM EVALUATING ACTIVITY A

SUGGEST IMPROVEMENTS TO THE QUESTIONS/PROCEDURE

- Were your questions clear or could they have been improved in some way?
- Could you have given more (or different) choices of answers?
- Do you wish that you had asked anything else?
- Are the results from open-ended questions difficult to analyse?
- How and where did participants complete the questions? Did they have long enough? Was it a suitable environment? Could they have been affected by other people or by social desirability?
- How did you select your participants? Could this method of selection be improved?

CONSIDER THE POSSIBLE EFFECTS OF THESE IMPROVEMENTS

For each of the improvements you have thought of, try to think what effect this might have had on your results:
- Would you be able to draw conclusions about anything else?
- Would you have improved reliability or validity?
- What effects might improved procedures or sampling methods have on your activity?

CONSIDER ISSUES OF RELIABILITY AND VALIDITY

- Reliability is defined as consistency. This means that you should expect to get the same responses if you asked the same people the same questions again. Do you think your questions gave you reliable results? How could you make your questionnaire more reliable?
- Validity is measuring what you thought you were measuring. For example, if you designed a questionnaire to measure study habits, are you really measuring your participants' study habits or what they think their study habits ought to be! How could you make this measure more valid?

EXPLAIN THE STRENGTHS AND WEAKNESSES OF QUESTIONNAIRES IN GENERAL

There are several strengths and weaknesses of questionnaires and you should be able to describe at least two of each:
- Strengths include the fact that you are asking people directly for information, rather than trying to infer something from their behaviour, the fact that you can collect large amounts of data

relatively quickly (and cheaply) and the fact that data collected from closed or fixed choice questions are relatively easy to analyse.

- Weaknesses include the fact that people may not tell you the truth, they may be subject to demand characteristics (giving you the answer that they think you want) or social desirability bias (giving you a socially acceptable answer), questions may not allow you to explore topics in detail, or may force people into answers which do not really reflect their opinion.

CONSIDER ETHICAL ISSUES RELATED TO THIS KIND OF RESEARCH.

- Questionnaires may be asking abut potentially distressing subject matter and this should be considered very carefully.
- Questioning people about illegal activities raises a number of ethical issues: you may be seen as condoning the behaviour by asking questions about it, the researcher may find themselves with an ethical dilemma (should they tell someone about illegal activities?) and there are also issues of confidentiality and data protection.

<table>
<tr>
<td>

☕ FOR CONSIDERATION

Was your research completely ethical? Could you make any improvements to the ethics of your research?

</td>
</tr>
</table>

REVISION

- Outline the aim of your activity.
- Give an example of one of your questions/self-reports.
- How did you select the participants for your study?
- Suggest one problem with this method of selection.
- Outline one of your findings.
- Describe an alternative way of finding out the same information.
- Identify one possible weakness in the way your questionnaire was designed or conducted and outline what you could have done to overcome this weakness.
- Suggest one improvement that could be made to the way you designed or conducted this activity.
- What do you think would be the effect of this improvement?
- Outline one strength of questionnaire/self-report measures in psychological research.
- Outline one weakness of questionnaire/self-report measures in psychological research.
- Outline one ethical issue that should be considered when conducting questionnaire/self-report research.
- If your questionnaire had been set up to investigate parents' use of corporal punishment, outline two problems that might be encountered with some of the answers.

ACTIVITY **B** I AN OBSERVATION

For this activity you need to choose something very simple to **observe** and design your own simple **coding scheme** to record your observations. You could observe how people spend their time in the common room or library, what food they choose to eat in the canteen or whether people are using litter bins or recycling bins.

As with Activity A, you could have **different conditions** for your observation, but this is not necessary. You could compare male and female behaviour, behaviour in the morning or afternoon or behaviour in the common room compared to the library.

You will need to consider how you are going to conduct your observation. You might choose to use a simple tally system, where you tick every time you see the behaviours on your list, or you may choose to observe an individual for a set amount of time recording their behaviour every 30 seconds or every minute.

SOME ADVICE FOR CONDUCTING ACTIVITY B

- Don't have too many categories – it will make your observation difficult to conduct as well as difficult to analyse.
- You don't need to observe for a very long period of time – half an hour or an hour would be fine.
- Don't spend too long getting the categories perfect – conduct the observation and then spend time thinking about the possible improvements.

DESIGNING YOUR OBSERVATION

Once you have decided what behaviours you are going to observe, you will also need to decide how you are going to conduct the observation. Some observations, such as use of recycling bins, will be simple tally charts where you record every time something happens. Other observations might be better conducted by recording what is happening every minute or every 30 seconds.

COMPLETING THE PRACTICAL WORK FOLDER

As with Activity A, keep this simple. Make sure that you can reproduce your coding schemes if asked to in the examination and that you can describe the categories fully.

There is no need to conduct statistical analysis of the data, it is enough to simply total categories or calculate percentages.

ACTIVITY A: AN OBSERVATION

State the aim of this activity:

The aim of this activity was to observe mobile phone use in the common room.

Describe the categories of behaviour that you observed and the rating or coding system that you used:

We observed the following:
• sex of the person

whether they were using their mobile phone for:
• talking
• texting
• playing games.

e.g.

Participant number	Male/female	talking	texting	games
1	M		X	
2	M	X		
3	F	X		

Details of sample:

Everyone in the common room between 10.30 and 11.00 am on a Tuesday morning. This totalled 83 people – 37 males and 46 females.

Outline the procedure:

The observers sat at a table near the entrance to the common room. There were four observers and they divided the common room into four equal areas for observation. Each person was observed and the observers recorded whether they were using a mobile phone and if so, whether they were talking, texting or playing games. The four observers then collated their results.

Summarise your findings

33 people were using mobile phones at the time of the observation:
Talking – 18 people (14 female and 4 male)
Texting – 10 people (6 female and 4 male)
Playing games – 5 people (0 female and 5 male)

HOT EXAM HINT

What other categories could you have included? Don't write these ideas in your folder, but consider them for the examination.

PREPARING FOR THE EXAM EVALUATING ACTIVITY B

SUGGEST IMPROVEMENTS TO THE CODING SCHEME/PROCEDURE

- Did you choose the right categories? Could you have added any extra categories or could you have sub-divided one or more of the categories that you had.
- Could you make any improvement to the way that you conducted the observation? This might include observing for longer, at different times of day, from a different observation point or at different time intervals.

CONSIDER THE POSSIBLE EFFECTS OF THESE IMPROVEMENTS

How might the improvements that you have identified above affect the results of your observation?

- You might be able to suggest that improvements would give a clearer picture of the behaviours under observation, allow you to compare morning and afternoon, and so on.

CONSIDER ISSUES OF RELIABILITY AND VALIDITY

In particular, you should consider **inter-rater reliability** and how to achieve this.

- Another word for **reliability** is consistency. In other words, would you get the same or similar results if you were to repeat your observation?
- Observational research should have good inter-rater reliability. This means that you should get the same results regardless of who is conducting the observation (using the same observational categories). Do you think that this would happen with your research? If two observers conducted the same observation they should have recorded the same results. You might be able to suggest improving the descriptions of each category so that all observers are clear about what each category means. It might also involve changing the way that you conducted the research. For example, there may have been too much to observe and you may have missed some of the behaviours that you were looking for.
- You can test for inter-rater reliability by **correlating** the scores of two observers. You would expect to find a high positive correlation.
- Validity is whether you were really testing (or observing) what you thought you were observing. Perhaps some of the behaviours should have been categorised in a different way. Perhaps if people knew that they were being observed, you were really observing how they thought they should behave in that particular situation rather than how they would behave if they did not think they were being observed.

EXPLAIN THE STRENGTHS AND WEAKNESSES OF OBSERVATIONAL TECHNIQUES IN GENERAL

- Observational research has many strengths. There is higher **ecological validity** if you are observing in the real world and lower **demand characteristics** if participants do not know that they are being observed.
- The weaknesses of observation include the **lack of control** over variables, which makes drawing cause and effect conclusions quite difficult and the fact that it is very difficult to **replicate** observational research.

CONSIDER ETHICAL ISSUES RELATED TO OBSERVATIONAL RESEARCH

- The main issue to consider is invasion of privacy/lack of consent.
- Do you think that researchers should be able to observe people without them knowing that they are taking part in psychological research?

FOR CONSIDERATION

How would you feel if you realised that someone had been observing you?

REVISION

- Outline the aim of your observation.
- Describe the coding scheme (or categories) that you used for your observation.
- Outline the procedure that you followed when carrying out your observation.
- Outline one of your findings.
- Outline one conclusion that can be drawn from your results.
- Suggest an alternative way of sampling/coding the behaviour that you were observing.
- What effect do you think that the above alternative would have on the validity of your results?
- What is meant by inter-rater reliability?
- How is inter-rater reliability measured?
- Suggest how your observation could be made more reliable.
- Suggest *two* improvements that could be made to your observation and the effects of these improvements.
- Identify one ethical issue that should be considered by researchers carrying out observational research.
- Outline one strength and one weakness of observational methods.
- A researcher wishes to observe the behaviour of children in hospital. Describe one ethical problem which the researcher might face and suggest how this might be overcome.

ACTIVITY C | COMPARISON OF DATA TO INVESTIGATE THE DIFFERENCE BETWEEN TWO CONDITIONS

For this activity you must have **two conditions** that you are comparing. This means that you will be most likely to use an experimental method. You could manipulate one variable and measure its effect. For example, you could investigate the effects of noise on attention by having participants complete a task in either a quiet room or a noisy room.

SOME ADVICE FOR CONDUCTING ACTIVITY C

- Don't have more than two conditions as this will only lead to confusion in the exam. You can always suggest other conditions when you are thinking about improvements.
- Keep participant numbers low – e.g. ten in each condition.
- Keep the task simple. You don't want to produce very complicated data which will be difficult to score and to analyse. You should also keep the tasks fairly short so that your participants do not get bored.

DESIGNING YOUR ACTIVITY

There are several different ways you could investigate the difference between two conditions. One type of experimental design is **independent measures** and this is when you have different participants in each of your conditions. An alternative design is **repeated measures** and this is where you have the same people taking part in each condition.

COMPLETING THE PRACTICAL WORK FOLDER

Make sure you have a clearly expressed **hypothesis** and **null hypothesis**. These should include both the independent and dependent variable.

Conduct a statistical test. This can be a very simple test such as the Sign test or Wilcoxon (for paired scores) or Mann Whitney (for independent scores). Ensure that you understand the relationship between calculated values, critical values and probability. Write a clear statement of significance explaining whether your hypothesis can be accepted or rejected and give the reasons why.

HOT EXAM HINT

The variable that is manipulated is the independent variable and the variable that is measured is the dependent variable. Your hypothesis should state clearly how you expect the independent variable to affect the dependent variable.

FOR CONSIDERATION

Several of the core studies compare two (or more) conditions. For examples look at Loftus and Palmer (Chapter 2), Samuel and Bryant (Chapter 3), Schachter and Singer (Chapter 4), Piliavin et al. (Chapter 5) and Hraba and Grant (Chapter 6).

Which other core studies compare different conditions?

KEY CONCEPT

The advantages of repeated measures are that you are comparing the same people (so you have reduced subject variability) and you also need fewer participants in total. However, some investigations would not be suitable for repeated measures as the participants are more likely to work out the aim of your investigation and this would lead to increased demand characteristics.

HOT EXAM HINT

Draw a graph summarising the data. The graph should be simple (comparisons of totals or means for each condition is far better than graphs that display all the raw scores). Calculate the mean, median, mode and range (or whichever are appropriate) for your data.

REMEMBER

An example of statement of significance:

'As the calculated value of U (5.5) was less than the critical value (10), I can accept my experimental hypothesis and reject my null hypothesis. This means that there is less than one chance in 20 that my results are due to chance and I conclude that people do remember word lists more effectively if they learn them in a quiet room rather than a noisy room.'

CD-ROM

Psychological Investigations:
Data analysis 1, 2 and 3

ACTIVITY C: COLLECTION OF DATA TO INVESTIGATE THE DIFFERENCE BETWEEN TWO CONDITIONS

State the hypothesis and null hypothesis for this activity:
HYPOTHESIS: Participants who chew gum while they are learning a list of words will recall more words than participants who are not chewing gum.
NULL HYPOTHESIS: Chewing gum will have no effect on recall.

Identify the variables:
IV – whether or not the participant is chewing gum while learning the word list.
DV – number of words recalled.

Describe the two conditions:
Condition A: participants are given a list of 20 randomly chosen two-syllable words (all nouns, e.g. basket, handbag, sausage) and given a piece of chewing gum to chew while learning the words.
Condition B: as Condition A, but without the chewing gum.

Details of sample:
20 participants – 10 in each group. No psychology students took part. Opportunity sample from common room.

Outline the design/procedure:
Independent measures design
10 participants in a quiet classroom – given word list and chewing gum. 2 minutes allowed to learn the word list and 2 minutes straight afterwards to recall the word list.
A second group of 10 participants were tested following this. They were given the word list and the same time to learn and recall the words.
1 mark was given for each correct word recalled.

Name the statistical test used to analyse the data:
Mann Whitney U test

What were the results of this analysis?
Calculated value of U = 3   Critical value for significance at 0.005 = 16
Therefore this is significant at $p < 0.005$ (1 in 200)

Conclusions/statements of significance relating to the hypothesis:
As the calculated value of U was lower than the critical value, the hypothesis can be supported and the null hypothesis rejected. Participants who are chewing gum while learning a list of words remember significantly more words than participants who are not allowed to chew gum.

Use this space to present data using tables, visual displays and verbal summaries:

	Condition A Chewing gum	Condition B No chewing gum
MEAN	12.5	9.4
MEDIAN	13	9
RANGE	6 (9–15)	7 (7–14)

You may attach a computer print out to this practical folder, or record your calculations here:

PREPARING FOR THE EXAM
EVALUATING ACTIVITY C

SUGGEST IMPROVEMENTS TO THE PROCEDURE AND THE LIKELY EFFECTS OF THESE IMPROVEMENTS

HOT EXAM HINT

Make sure that you can describe the strengths and weaknesses of both independent measures designs and repeated measures designs.

- What **weaknesses** might there have been in the way that you conducted this investigation? These might include the environment in which participants were tested, the materials that you used or the instructions that you gave the participants. How could you overcome these weaknesses?
- What would be the likely effects of these improvements? Would they allow you to draw stronger conclusions (for example ensuring that each group had exactly the same instructions would make any effects you found even more likely to be due to your independent variable).

SUGGEST ALTERNATIVE WAYS OF MEASURING THE DEPENDENT VARIABLE

- Make sure you know what the dependent variable is for your investigation. This is the variable that you measured and you would have had to decide how to measure this. This is called **operationalisation**. For example, you may have decided to 'operationalise' memory as the number of words that could be remembered from a word list, but there are literally hundreds of ways in which memory could have been measured.
- Try to think of at least **one alternative way** of measuring your dependent variable and consider the possible effects of this alternative. Do you think the alternative is better than the way you chose originally? Why?

CONSIDER ISSUES RELATING TO THE SAMPLE

- How was your sample selected? What are the strengths and weaknesses of this type of selection?
- Suggest one other sample that could be used in this investigation and explain how this might affect the results.

DESCRIBE THE STRENGTHS AND WEAKNESSES OF THE EXPERIMENTAL METHOD AND THE DIFFERENT TYPES OF EXPERIMENTAL DESIGN

- Generally speaking, experimental methods tend to have **high levels of control**. The more variables that are controlled, the easier it is to draw conclusions about the effect of your independent variable on your dependent variable.

- Weaknesses of experimental methods include the fact that they often lack **ecological validity** as they are conducted in artificial conditions and they may be **reductionist**, for example defining memory simply in terms of how many words can be recalled from a list.

CONSIDER ETHICAL ISSUES RELATED TO THIS ACTIVITY

- Do you think that your research followed the ethical guidelines in full?
- Did you ensure that all participants gave informed consent, were aware of their right to withdraw from the investigation, and were fully debriefed?

REVISION

- State the research hypothesis for your investigation.
- State the null hypothesis for your investigation.
- Identify the independent and dependent variables in your investigation.
- What were the two conditions of your investigation?
- Describe how the dependent variable was measured.
- Suggest an alternative way of measuring this variable.
- Outline the procedure that you followed.
- Sketch an appropriately labelled graph displaying your data.
- Outline one conclusion that can be drawn from this graph.
- Name the statistical test that was used to analyse your data and the results of this analysis.
- Outline the conclusion that you reached in relation to your null hypothesis.
- What is meant by a repeated (or related) measures design?
- Outline one advantage of this design.
- What is meant by an independent (or unrelated) measures design?
- Outline one advantage of this design.
- What design did you use for your investigation?
- Give one advantage of using this design.

ACTIVITY D | CORRELATION

Correlation is a **statistical technique** which measures the relationship between two variables. Correlation involves measuring two variables rather than manipulating one and measuring another and this means that you cannot draw conclusions about cause and effect from correlations – only about the relationship between them. An example of a correlation would be to investigate the relationship between the numbers of hours sleep someone has had and their score on some sort of reaction time task.

SOME ADVICE FOR CONDUCTING ACTIVITY D

- Choose **independent measures** that are simple to measure. You don't want to have to spend hours scoring lengthy tests.
- Why not overlap this activity with Activity A? If you asked people for a rating of how much they liked a particular subject, you could correlate this with how much time they say they spend doing homework for this subject.

DESIGNING YOUR CORRELATION

Make sure you understand the difference between a positive and a negative correlation. A positive correlation is a relationship between variables where as one increases, the other increases (or as one decreases, the other decreases). You might expect a positive correlation between the temperature and the amount of ice cream people buy! A negative correlation is a relationship between variables where as one increases the other decreases. For example, you might expect a negative correlation between the temperature and the number of hot-water bottles that people buy!

COMPLETING THE PRACTICAL WORK FOLDER

As with Activity C, spend some time constructing hypotheses for the correlation. Ensure that you have a correlational hypothesis and not a prediction of difference.

Describe how each of the variables were measured. In this kind of research the variables are referred to as independent measures. You do not have an independent variable and a dependent variable as you are not manipulating anything.

Draw a scattergram. Conduct a statistical analysis of your data (most commonly Spearmans rho or Pearsons Product Moment). It is acceptable to use a computer statistical package to do this. Write a clear statement of significance.

HOT EXAM HINT

Be very careful with this activity. You are not allowed to ask people for sensitive or personal information and this would include asking them for test scores or GCSE results. Imagine how you might feel if you were asked to call out this sort of information in front of lots of people.

FOR CONSIDERATION

Are you predicting a positive correlation or a negative correlation?

FOR CONSIDERATION

An example correlational hypothesis:

'There will be a positive correlation between the number of hours revision done for a test and the score achieved on that test'.

ACTIVITY D COLLECTION OF DATA INVOLVING TWO INDEPENDENT MEASURES AND ANALYSIS USING A TEST OF CORRELATION

<u>State the hypothesis and null hypothesis for this activity:</u>
HYPOTHESIS: There will be a significant positive correlation between a participant's self-rating of alertness and their score on a word search task.
NULL HYPOTHESIS: There will be no significant correlation between a participant's self-rating of alertness and their score on a word search task.

<u>Describe the two variables and how they were measured:</u>
Self rating of alertness: this was measured on a 1–10 scale where 1 = very tired and 10 = very alert.
Score on word search task: number of words found on a word search task within 3 minutes

<u>Details of sample:</u>
10 students (5 male and 5 female) No psychology students took part. Opportunity sample from common room. All aged 16–18 years old.

<u>Summarise the procedure:</u>
Participants were asked to complete a self-rating of alertness by circling a number between 1 and 10 on a scale. When these were completed they were asked to complete a word search which involved finding the titles of 20 television programmes. They were given 3 minutes to complete this task.

<u>Use this space to present data using tables, visual displays and verbal summaries:</u>

Alertness	No. of words found
5	8
6	10
7	12
7	10
7	12
8	12
8	14
8	12
9	16
9	16
MEAN	**MEAN**
7.4	12.2

<u>Name the statistical test used to analyse your data:</u>
Spearman's rank

<u>What were the results of the statistical analysis?</u>
Rho = 0.91
significant at 0.005 (1 in 200)

<u>Conclusions/statements of significance relating to the hypothesis:</u>
As the calculated value is larger than the critical value, the hypothesis can be supported and the null hypothesis rejected. There is a significant correlation between participants' self-rating of alertness and their scores on a word search.

HOT EXAM HINT

How else could you measure these variables? Don't write your ideas in your folder, but consider this for the examination.

PREPARING FOR THE EXAM EVALUATING ACTIVITY D

SUGGEST IMPROVEMENTS TO THE MEASUREMENT OF VARIABLES/PROCEDURE

- For each of your independent measures, consider any **weaknesses** that there may have been in the way that you measured them. Were your measurements **reliable**? Were they **valid**? Were there any problems in the way that you conducted this investigation, such as different participants being tested in very different conditions?
- Try to identify one **improvement** for each weakness that you have identified.

CONSIDER THE EFFECTS OF THESE IMPROVEMENTS

- How would your suggested improvements affect the results of your investigation?
- Do you think you have made the measurements more reliable?
- Have you reduced any **demand characteristics**?

CONSIDER ALTERNATIVE WAYS OF MEASURING THE VARIABLES

Your answers to this may well overlap with your answers to the questions above, but it is worth making sure that you can think of alternatives for both variables.

For each variable that you measured, try to think of an alternative way of getting the same information. For example, rather than asking for the number of hours' sleep that someone had, you could ask them to rate on a 1–10 scale how alert they feel.

CONSIDER ISSUES RELATING TO THE SAMPLE

- How was your sample selected? What are the strengths and weaknesses of this type of selection?
- Suggest one other sample that could be used in this investigation and explain how this might affect the results.

EXPLAIN THE STRENGTHS AND WEAKNESSES OF CORRELATION

The main strength of correlation is that it allows you to identify relationships between variables **without manipulation**. This might be useful if the variables that you are interested in are difficult, impossible or unethical to manipulate.

The main weakness is that correlation does **not imply causation**. Identifying a relationship between two variables does not mean that one causes the other. You have simply demonstrated that they are related in some way.

REVISION

- Identify the two variables in your investigation.
- Describe how one of the variables was measured.
- Suggest an alternative way of measuring one of the variables and suggest what effect this alternative might have on the results of your investigation.
- Using an appropriately labelled scattergram, sketch the data that you collected.
- Outline one conclusion that can be drawn from this scattergram.
- Name the statistical test that you used to analyse your data and the results of this analysis.
- Explain, in relation to the null hypothesis, the conclusion that you reached.
- What is meant by a positive correlation?
- What is meant by a negative correlation?
- If a researcher found a positive correlation between stress levels and the number of cups of coffee drunk, could they conclude that drinking coffee makes people stressed? Explain your answer.
- If a researcher found a positive correlation between the amount of violent television watched and aggressive behaviour, could it be concluded that watching violent television causes aggressive behaviour? Explain your answer.

AN INTRODUCTION TO STATISTICS

Whenever we carry out research in psychology, we generate data. These data need to be understood and interpreted. **Descriptive statistics** allow us to describe and summarise data. **Inferential statistics** allow us to make inferences and draw conclusions about our results.

DESCRIPTIVE STATISTICS

Measures of central tendency (mean, median, mode)

The **mean** is calculated by adding all the scores together and then dividing by the number of scores. This is a useful statistic as it takes all the scores into account but can be misleading if there are one or more **extreme scores** all in the same direction.

The **median** is the mid point that separates the higher 50 per cent of scores from the lower 50 per cent of scores. This is a more useful measure than the mean when there are extreme scores or a **skewed distribution**. It does not, however, work well with small data sets and can be affected by any alteration of the central values.

The **mode** is the score that occurs most often. It is possible to have more than one mode; a set of data with two modes is called **bimodal,** and a set of data with more than two modes is called **multimodal.** The mode is useful where other scores may be meaningless. It may make more sense to know the most common responses to a question rather than the mean response.

Measures of variability or dispersion

The **range** is the difference between the smallest and largest number in a set of scores. It is a fairly crude measure of variability as one very high or very low score can distort the data.

The **standard deviation (SD)** is a statistical measure of dispersion. It tells us how much, on average, scores differ from the mean score. A large SD tells us that the spread of scores is wide, a small SD tells us that all the scores are clustered together around the mean.

INFERENTIAL STATISTICS

When we analyse data we are asking: 'Which of our hypotheses offers the best explanation for our results?'. We cannot prove one hypothesis to be correct, but we can make an intelligent guess about which one is the more likely explanation. This is called an **inference**. We want to assess the **probability** that our results could be due to chance factors. To assess this probability we use inferential statistics.

FOR CONSIDERATION

IS THE MEAN A USEFUL FIGURE TO CALCULATE?

The mean of 8, 10, 10, 12, 60 would not be a very helpful figure!

The mean of 100, 101, 99, 102, 98, 100 is 100.

The mean of 100, 40, 120, 60, 180, 100 is also 100 – the mean in this case would not reflect the very different distribution of scores.

REMEMBER

The median of 2, 4, 6, 8, 19 is 6.

FOR CONSIDERATION

IS THE MODE A USEFUL FIGURE TO CALCULATE?

The mode has its limitations and when there are only a few scores representing each value, very small changes can dramatically alter the mode. For example:

3, 6, 8, 9, 10, 10 – mode = 10
3, 3, 6, 8, 9, 10 – mode = 3

The mode will always be a value that actually exists in your data, which may not be true of other measures of central tendency.

KEY CONCEPT

When we carry out a psychological investigation we usually have *two* hypotheses:

- the **null hypothesis**, which states that the results will be due to **chance**
- the **experimental (alternate) hypothesis**, which predicts that the results are due to the **manipulation of the variable** being studied.

For example, if we carry out a study on the effect of an audience on reaction time, we might obtain the following results:
Average time to sort a pack of playing cards into suits
- with an audience – 38 seconds
- without an audience – 34 seconds.

We need to know whether this four seconds' difference in performance is due to the effect of the audience, or whether it is due to the variation caused by chance effects. Statistics tell us the probability that the null hypothesis could explain our results, that is, the probability that our results are due to chance. It is an **academic convention** in psychology that we accept the null hypothesis as the best explanation of our results unless there is only a **5 per cent probability** (or less) of the results being due to chance. This written as: p < 0.05.

If our statistical test tells us that the probability of the results being due to chance is less than 5 per cent, then we can REJECT the NULL hypothesis and ACCEPT the EXPERIMENTAL (alternate) hypothesis.

However, we have not proved that the audience caused an increase in reaction time. We have **inferred a causal link** and there is a possibility (5 per cent or one in 20) that we are wrong and the results simply occurred by chance. In other words, we can be 95 per cent confident of our conclusion. Sometimes we need to be more than 95 per cent confident. Would you take a new medicine if the doctor said they were 95 per cent sure that it had no harmful side effects? In this case, we would use a **more stringent significance level**, and only reject the null hypothesis if we are 99 per cent confident (p < 0.01) or even 99.9 per cent confident (p < 0.001).

REMEMBER

If p < 0.05, this means that there is a one in 20 probability that the results occurred by chance.
If p < 0.01, this means that there is a one in 100 probability that the results occurred by chance. This gives you a higher level of confidence in rejecting the null hypothesis.
If p < 0.005, this is equal to a probability of one in 200.
If p < 0.001, this is equal to a probability of one in 1000.

Whatever statistical test you use, you will calculate a **value** that has to be interpreted using a **significance table**. There are specific significance tables for different tests. Interpreting the value will give you a level of significance, that is, a probability that the results occurred by chance.

We can never be 100 per cent sure that our results are not due to chance; it is possible that we might reject our null hypothesis and accept our experimental (alternate) hypothesis when the results were, in fact, simply a chance occurrence. This is termed a **Type 1 error**. If we were to accept the null hypothesis and reject the experimental (alternate) hypothesis when in fact the results were due to our experimental manipulation, this would be termed a **Type 2 error**.

The 0.05 significance level is commonly used in psychology as it is thought to offer the best balance between the risk of making a Type 1 and a Type 2 error.

KEY CONCEPTS

confounding variable A variable that causes a change in the dependent variable but which was not the IV of the study. If confounding variables are not controlled, they make conclusions regarding the effect of the IV on the DV very difficult to reach.

control group A group used for comparison with an experimental group. Control groups do not experience the manipulation of the IV.

correlation coefficient A number which expresses the strength of a relationship between two variables and which is calculated using statistical tests such as Spearmans rho. Correlation coefficients are between –1 (strong negative correlation) and +1 (strong positive correlation).

demand characteristics Clues or 'cues' in any research situation which suggest to participants how they should be behaving.

dependent variable (DV) The variable that is measured.

hypothesis The prediction that is made about the effect of the IV on the DV. May be referred to as the alternate or experimental hypothesis.

independent measures design A design using different participants in each condition of the experiment.

independent variable (IV) The variable that is manipulated.

inter-rater reliability The amount of agreement between two observers using the same observation schedule and observing the same participants.

mean One measure of central tendency. The score that is achieved when you add up the scores and divide by the number of scores.

median Another measure of central tendency. The median is calculated by listing all the scores in ascending order and finding the middle one.

mode The most commonly occurring score.

negative correlation A relationship between variables in which they move in different directions, that is, as one variable increases, the other decreases.

null hypothesis The 'no-effect' hypothesis. This is a statement which says that the IV will have no effect on the DV (or that any effect will be due to change that is too small to be significant).

order effects The effect of taking part in more than one condition of experimental research which may mean that participants become better at tasks (practice effects) or worse at tasks (boredom effects).

positive correlation A relationship between variables in which they both move in the same direction, that is, as one variable increases, so does the other or as one variable decreases, so does the other.

range The distance between the highest and the lowest score.

reliability Consistency of measurement.

repeated measures design A design using the same participants in each condition of the experiment.

validity Whether your measurement is measuring what you think it is measuring.

USEFUL RESOURCES

BOOKS

Coolican, H. (1992) *Research Methods and Statistics in Psychology*, Hodder & Stoughton.

Searle, A. (1999) *Introducing Research and Data in Psychology: A guide to Methods and Analysis*, Routledge Modular Psychology Series, Routledge.

The Philip Allan *Updates Student Guide* mentioned in the Useful Resources section in Chapter 1 is specifically written for this module and includes guidance on conducting each of the activities and preparing for the examination.

AUTHOR INDEX

Index to Authors of Core Studies and recommended books

Full references to publication data appear on the lowest numbered (and thus the first quoted) page under each reference

Aronson, E
The Social Animal
Eliot Aronson (1976)   124

Bandura A
Transmission of aggression through imitation of aggressive models
A Bandura, D Ross and D A Ross (1961)   2, 43, 50–55

Banks, W C
A Study of prisoners and guards in a simulated prison
C Haney, W C Banks and P G Zimbardo (1973)   3, 99, 106–111

Baron-Cohen, S
Does the autistic child have a "theory of mind"?
S Baron-Cohen, A M Leslie and U Frith (1985)   2, 15, 28–33

Berry R
Freud: A Beginner's Guide
R Berry (2000)   68

Bryant, P
Asking only one question in the conservation experiment
J Samuel and P Bryant (1984)   2, 43, 44–49

Buchsbaum, M
Brain abnormalities in murderers indicated by positron emission tomography
A Raine, M Buschsbaum and L LaCasse 3, 71, 90–95

Carter, R
Mapping the Mind
R Carter (1998)   96

Cialdini, R
Influence: Science and Practice
Robert Cialdini (1993)   124

Cleckley, H
A case of multiple personality
C H Thigen and H Cleckley

(1954)   3, 127, 146–151
The Three Faces of Eve
C Thigpen and H Cleckley (1992)   152

Dement W
The Promise of Sleep
W Dement and C Vaughn (2000)   96
The relation of eye movements during sleep to dream activity: An objective method for the study of dreaming
W Dement and N Kleitman (1957)   3, 71, 78–83

Deregowski, J B
Pictorial perception and culture
J B Deregowski (1972)   2, 15, 22–27

Donaldson, M
Children's Minds
M Donaldson (1984)   68
Human Minds: An Exploration
M Donaldson (1992)   68

Freud S
Analysis of a phobia of a five-year-old boy
S Freud (1909)   2, 43, 62–67

Frith, U
Does the autistic child have a "theory of mind"?
S Baron-Cohen, A M Leslie and U Frith (1985)   2, 15, 28–33

Gardner, B T
Teaching sign language to a chimpanzee
R A Gardner and B T Gardner (1969)   2, 15, 34–49

Gardner, R A
Teaching sign language to a chimpanzee

R A Gardner and B T Gardner (1969)   2, 15, 34–49

Gould, S J
A nation of morons
S J Gould (1982)   3, 127, 128–133

Grant G
Black is beautiful: A re-examination of racial preference and identification
J Hraba and G Grant (1970)   3, 127, 134–139

Green, S
Principles of BioPsychology
S Green (1994)   96

Gross R
Psychology: The Science of Mind of Behaviour
R Gross (2001)   40, 68, 96, 124, 152

Haney, C
A Study of prisoners and guards in a simulated prison
C Haney, W C Banks and P G Zimbardo (1973)   3, 99, 106–111

Hodges J
Social and family relationships of ex-institutional adolescents
J Hodges and B Tizard (1989b)   2, 43, 56–61

Hraba, J
Black is beautiful: A re-examination of racial preference and identification
J Hraba and G Grant (1970)   3, 127, 134–139

Keyes, D
The Minds of Billy Milligan
D Keyes (1995)   152

Kleitman N
The relation of eye movements during sleep to dream activity:

An objective method for the study of dreaming
W Dement and N Kleitman (1957)   3, 71, 78–83

LaCasse, L
Brain abnormalities in murderers indicated by positron emission tomography
A Raine, M Buschsbaum and L LaCasse   3, 71, 90–95

Leslie, A M
Does the autistic child have a "theory of mind"?
S Baron-Cohen, A M Leslie and U Frith (1985)   2, 15, 28–33

Loftus, E F
Eye Witness Testimony
E F Loftus (1996)   40
Reconstruction of automobile destruction: An example of the interaction between language and memory
E F Loftus and J C Palmer (1974)   2, 15, 16–21

Masson, J
Final Analysis, the Making and unmaking of a Psychoanalyst
J Masson (1992)   68
The Assault on Truth, Freud and Child Sexual Abuse
J Masson (1992)   68

Milgram, S
Behavioural study of obedience
Stanley Milgram (1963)   3, 99, 100–105
Obedience to Authority
Stanley Milgram (1974)   124

Moxon D
Memory
D Moxon (2000)   40

O'Connell, S
Mind Reading: How We Learn to Love and Lie
S O'Connel (1997)   40

Palmer, J C
Reconstruction of automobile destruction: An example of the interaction between language and memory
E F Loftus and J C Palmer (1974)   2, 15, 16–21

Piliavan, I M
Good Samaritanism: An underground phenomenon?
I M Piliavan, J A Rodin and J Piliavan   3, 99, 112–117

Piliavan, J
Good Samaritanism: An underground phenomenon?
I M Piliavan, J A Rodin and J Piliavan   3, 99, 112–117

Pinker, S
How the Mind Works
S Pinker (1997)   96

Prendergast, M
Victims of Memory: Incest Accusations and Shattered Lives
M Prendergast (1997)   152

Raine, A
Brain abnormalities in murderers indicated by positron emission tomography
A Raine, M Buschsbaum and L LaCasse   3, 71, 90–95

Rodin, J A
Good Samaritanism: An underground phenomenon?
I M Piliavan, J A Rodin and J Piliavan   3, 99, 112–117

Rosenham, D L
On being sane in insane places
D L Rosenham (1973)   3, 127, 140–145

Ross D
Transmission of aggression through imitation of aggressive models
A Bandura, D Ross and D A Ross (1961)   2, 43, 50–55

Ross S A
Transmission of aggression through imitation of aggressive models
A Bandura, D Ross and D A Ross (1961)   2, 43, 50–55

Samuel, J
Asking only one question in the conservation experiment
J Samuel and P Bryant (1984)   2, 43, 44–49

Schachter, S
Cognitive, social and physiological determinants of emotional state
S Schachter and J E Singer (1962)   3, 71, 72–77

Schreiber, F R
Sybil
F R Schreiber (1974)   152

Singer, J E
Cognitive, social and physiological determinants of emotional state
S Schachter and J E Singer (1962)   3, 71, 72–77

Sperry, R W
Hemisphere disconnection and unity in consciousness
R W Sperry (1968)   3, 71, 84–89

Tajfel, H
Experiments in intergroup discrimination
H Tajfe (1970)   3, 99, 118–123

Temple, C
The Brain: An introduction to the Psychology of the Human Brain and Behaviour
C Temple (1993)   96

Thigpen, C H
A case of multiple personality
C H Thigpen and H Cleckley (1954)   3, 127, 146–151
The Three Faces of Eve
C H Thigpen and H Cleckley (1992)   152

Tizard B
Social and family relationships of ex-institutional adolescents
J Hodges and B Tizard (1989b)   2, 43, 56–61

Vaughn, C
The Promise of Sleep
W Dement and C Vaughn (2000)   96

Zimbardo, P G
A Study of prisoners and guards in a simulated prison
C Haney, W C Banks and P G Zimbardo (1973)   3, 99, 106–111

INDEX

A

abnormal social development 56
abnormality 127, 140–145
abnormality definitions 140–141
accommodation 44
activation synthesis model 79
activities
  A: questions etc. 155, 156–159
  B: an observation 155, 160–163
  C: data comparison 155, 164–167
  causation 171
  coding scheme 160, 162
  control levels 166
  correlation 168–171
  D: correlation 155, 168–171
  data collecting 155
  data comparison 164–167
  demand characteristics 164, 170
  dependent variable 164, 167
  difference between two conditions 164–167
  ecological validity 167
  ethical issues 159, 163, 167
  hypothesis 164, 165, 168, 169
  independent measures 164, 168
  independent variable 164
  Mann Whitney test 164
  null hypothesis 164, 165, 168, 169
  observation 160–163
  operationalisation 166
  practical work folder 157, 160, 164–165, 168–169
  questioning people 156–159
  questionnaires 156–159
  reductionist 167
  reliability 158, 162, 170
  repeated measures 164
  self-reports 156–159
  Sign test 164
  significance 164, 165
  validity 158, 162, 170
  Wilcoxon test 164

adrenalin 74
affection 58–59
affectionless psychopathy 56
after event information 17, 18–19
aggression arousal 52
aggressive behaviour 43, 50–55, 71, 90–95
alternative hypothesis 173
American Sign Language (ASL) 36
Ames room distortion 23
Ameslan 36
amygdala 72, 90, 93
anecdotal evidence 26
anger condition 74–75
Army alpha test 130
Army beta test 130
ASL 36
'asocial' state 28
Asperger's syndrome 28–29
assimilation 44
assumptions, power of 16
attachment figure 61
authoritarian personality 118
authority power 99, 100–105
autism 28–29
autistic children
  false belief task 15, 28–33
  theory of mind 29, 30–31, 33
available explanation 74

B

behaviour aggression effect 43, 50–55
behavioural observations 76
behaviourism 50
belief question 31
beliefs 23
bimodal data 172
bio-physiological *see* physiological approach
biochemical theories 90
biological explanations of aggression 90
biological factors 128
'blank slate' minds 44

blind obedience 99, 100–105
brain
  aggression abnormalities 71, 90–95
  Broca's area 84–85
  hemispheres 71, 84–89, 92, 93
  'pictures' hemisphere 84
  Wernicke's area 85
  'words' hemisphere 84
British Psychological Society 105
Broca's area 84–85
bystander apathy 112
bystander behaviour 112
bystander research 99, 112–117

C

Cannon-Bard theory 73
'carpentered environment' 23
case studies 7, 38, 150
castration anxiety 63, 64
causal link 173
causation 171
cause and effect relationships 122
central tendency measures 172
centration 45
childhood seduction 62
children in institutions 43, 56–61
chimpanzee and sign language 15, 34–39
Chomsky 35
chronological age 128
classification systems 141
closed questions 7
coding scheme 160, 162
cognitive appraisal of situation 71, 72–77
cognitive approach 13–40
  books 40
  core studies outline 15
  definition 15
  strengths 40
  weaknesses 40
  websites 40
cognitive development 43, 44–49
Cognitive Labelling theory 73

communications impairment 28
confidentiality 11
confiding 59
conformity to social norms 90
consent 10
conservation skills 43, 44–49
consolidation prevention 17
control levels 166
controlled conditions 20
corpus callosum 71, 84–89
correlation 81, 168–171
critical belief question 31
cross-cultural research 23
cross-sectional designs 60
cultural bias 129

D
data collecting activities 155
data collection 132
data comparison 164–167
data interpretation 132
DD 146
death instinct 90
debriefing 10–11
deception 10
deception guideline 105
deindividuation 90
demand characteristics 17, 19, 20, 139, 164, 170
dependent variable 164, 167
depersonalisation 143
depth cues 24
descriptive statistics 172
desirable behaviours 140
determinism 8
developmental approach 41–68
  books 68
  core studies outline 43
  definition 43
  strengths 68
  weaknesses 68
  websites 68
Devlin Committee 17
diagnostic interviews 107
DID 127, 146–151
difference between two conditions 164–167
differentiation 37
Diffusion of Responsibility hypothesis 99, 112–117
discrimination 99, 118–123
dispersion measures 172

dispositional hypothesis 106
dissociative disorders (DD) 146
Dissociative Identity Disorder (DID) 127, 146–151
Down's syndrome 30
Down's syndrome children, false belief task 15, 28–33
dreaming 71, 78–83
  interpretations 79
  recall 80–83
DSM 141

E
ecological validity 8, 20–21, 32–33, 48, 49, 54, 82–83, 89, 104–105, 110, 116, 122, 144, 167
EEG readings 91, 148, 149
egocentric 45
electroencephalogram (EEG) readings 91, 148, 149
emotion 23
  cognitive processing 71, 72–77
  physiological arousal 71, 72–77
emotional environment 74
engram 16
environmental factors 128, 150–151
epilepsy 71, 84–89
epinephrine 74
Ethical Guidelines 105
ethical implications 95
ethical issues 54, 67, 167
ethics 8, 10–11
ethics of studies 39, 49, 55, 77, 95, 105, 116–117, 144, 151
ethnocentric bias 8
ethnocentrism 26–27, 123, 133, 139
ethology 90
eugenics 129, 131, 133
euphoria condition 74–75
'Eve' 127, 146–151
evolutionary theory 79
examinations
  core studies 1: 4
  core studies 2: 4–5
  practical investigations/work folder 5
  psychological investigations 5
expectations 16
experimental methods

field experiments 6
  laboratory experiments
  natural experiments 6
extreme scores 172
eye-witness testimony 17–21

F
false belief task
  autistic children 15, 28–33
  Down's syndrome children 15, 28–33
  normal children 15, 28–33
familiarity with tests 129
family relationships 58
field experiments 6, 116, 117, 142, 144
Freud, Sigmund 62–67
Freudian theory 90
frontal lobotomy 73
Frustration-Aggression theory 90

G
genetic factors 128
genetic predisposition 150–151
guards and prisoners study 99, 106–111

H
Hans study 64–67
highly controlled laboratory (quasi) experiment 94
Hole, The 107
Holocaust 100–101
horses phobia 64, 66
hypothesis 164, 165, 168, 169

I
ICD 141
imitative habits 52–53
imitative powers 36
immigration debate in USA 130–131
impairments triad 28
impossible trident 25
in-group 99, 118–123
in-group choices 120
independent measures 164, 168
independent measures experimental design 48
independent variable 164
individual differences approach 125–152

...utline 127
...7

... 152
...osites 152
individual explanation of
    behaviour 105, 111, 145
individual explanations 8–9
individual spoken test 130
infantile sexuality 62–63
inferential statistics 172–173
informed consent 10, 107
informed consent guideline 105
ink blot test 148
innate skills 23
insanity 127, 140–145
institutions for children 43, 56–61
intelligence
    concept 128
    cultural bias 129
    environmental factors 128
    genetic factors 128
    motivation 129
    quotient (IQ) 128–129
intelligence tests 127, 128–132
    administration 131
    Army alpha test 130
    Army beta test 130
    background 128–129
    familiarity 129
    individual spoken test 130
    IQ 128–129
    reliability 133
    validity 133
inter-cultural communication 24
inter-group choices 120
inter-group discrimination
    strategy 120
interference 17
interview methods 60
IQ 128–129

J
James-Lange theory 72, 73
'Jane' 149
juries 17

K
Kanner's syndrome 29
King, Martin Luther 135
Koro 140

L
laboratory experiments 6, 20,
    54, 82, 94, 104
language
    communication 35
    definition 34–35
    learning 34–35
    skills 37
    structure 35
language acquisition device 35
leading questions 15, 16–21, 64
learning by association 50
learning from environment 50
left hemisphere of brain 71,
    84–89, 92
libido 62–63
'lifespan' of research 139
limbic system 72, 90, 93
long-term memory 16
longitudinal study 57, 60

M
magnetic resonance imaging
    (MRI) 91
Mann Whitney test 164
maternal deprivation 56
maximum difference strategy
    121
maximum fairness strategy 120
maximum in-group profit
    strategy 121
maximum joint profit strategy
    120, 121
mean 172
media images 51
median 172
memory
    after event information 18–19
    factors affecting 16–17
    leading questions 15, 16–21
    stores 16
    time lasting 16
    trace 16
memory question 31
mental age 128
mental illness 127, 140–145
mental structure re-organisation
    79
methods 6–7
mind-blindness 29
minimal group 119
MMR vaccine 29

mode 172
modelling 50
monotropic bond 56
motivation 17, 23, 129
MPD 127, 146–151
MRI 91
Muller-Lyer illusion 23
multimodal data 172
multiple personality disorder
    (MPD) 127, 146–151
mundane realism 107
murderers 71, 90–95

N
naming question 31
native intellectual ability 131
natural experiments 6
nature-nurture debate 9, 27, 38,
    55, 61, 95, 128, 133, 150–151
Nazi party 100–101
neurological theories 90
neurophysiology of aggression
    90–91
non-aggressive see aggressive
non-REM sleep see rapid eye
    movements sleep
normal children, false belief task
    15, 28–33
'not guilty by insanity' pleas
    92–93
null hypothesis 164, 165, 168,
    169, 173
nurture see nature-nurture debate

O
obedience to authority 99,
    100–105
object permanence 45
observation 160–163
observational methods 6
observational research 11
Oedipus complex 43, 62–67
operant conditioning 34, 50
operationalisation 166
opposite-sex behaviour 52
order effects 48
out-group 99, 118–123
out-group choices 120

P
paradoxical sleep 78
participant observation 142, 144

pathological prison syndrome 109
perception 22–23
perception of events 19
perceptual set 22–23
persistent differences 24
personality tests 107
PET scans 71, 90–95
physiological approach 69–96
  books 96
  core studies outline 71
  definition 71
  strengths 96
  weaknesses 96
  websites 96
physiological process of seeing 22
Piaget 44–45
pictures as universal language 15, 22–27
'pictures' hemisphere of brain 84
placebo 74
political context of research 139
positive reinforcement 34
Positron emission tomography (PET) scans 71, 90–95
power of authority figure 99, 100–105
powerlessness 143
practical work/investigations folder 5, 157, 160, 164–165, 168–169
prejudice 118
prisoners and guards study 99, 106–111
probability 172–173
projective tests 150
protection from harm guideline 105
protection of participants 11
pseudopatients 142, 145
psychiatric diagnosis 141
psychiatric diagnosis doubts 145
psycho-sexual development 62–65
psychological investigations 153–171
psychological process of perceiving 22
psychology
  case studies 7

ethics 10–11
experimental methods 6
methods 6–7
observational methods 6
questioning people 6–7
review articles 7
themes 8–9
psychometric tests 132, 150
psychometrics 9
psychopathological context 142
punishment, effect on learning 101

Q
qualitative and quantitative data 26, 38, 54–55, 60–61, 88–89, 110, 144, 150
qualitative data 9, 67
quantitative data 9, 20, 32, 48–49, 76, 82, 94, 104, 122, 132, 138
quasi-experimental design 32, 88
quasi-experimental method 138
questioning people 6–7, 156–159
questionnaire methods 60
questionnaires 156–159

R
racial awareness 127, 134–139
racial preference 127, 134–139
racial self-identification 134
racism 131, 133
random allocation to conditions 76
range 172
rapid eye movements (REM) sleep 71, 78–83
Realistic Conflict Theory 118–119
reality question 31
reductionism 9, 123, 167
reductionist study 95
'refrigerator' parenting 29
regression 148
reinforcement 9, 34, 38–39, 55, 111, 145
reliability 9, 117, 141, 145, 158, 162, 170
REM sleep 71, 78–83
repeated measures 164
repetitive behaviour 28
replication of research 48, 138

repression 17, 148
response bias factors 18–1.
response strategies 120–121
restoration theory 79
review articles 7
Rhesus monkey 56
right hemisphere of brain 71, 84–89, 92, 93
right to withdraw guideline 105
Rorschach test 148
'royal road to the unconscious' 79

S
Sally-Anne task 30–31
same-sex behaviour 52
sample representation 21, 48, 54, 60, 76, 82, 88, 94, 110, 116, 122, 132, 138, 150
sanity 127, 140–145
schemata 44, 79
schizophrenia 142–143
'scientific racism' 133
seeing process 22
segregation in USA 135
self-reporting 60, 75, 156–159
self-selected sample 104
sensory memory 16
shaping signs 36
shock generator 102
short-term memory 16
sibling relationships 58
sign combinations 37
sign language and chimpanzee 15, 34–39
Sign test 164
sign transfers 37
significance 164, 165
significance level 173
significance table 173
situational cognitions 75
situational explanation of behaviour 8–9, 49, 77, 105, 111, 145
Sizemore, Christine 127, 146–151
skewed distribution 172
sleep 71, 78–83
  brainwave patterns 78
  stages 78
social approach 97–124
  books 124
  core studies outline 99

9

4

24

...research 139

...control 9, 133, 145

social desirability bias 76

social desirability of research 60

social factors 128

Social Identity Theory 118–119

social interaction impairment 28

Social Learning theory 50–51, 90

social norms conformity 90

social relationships 43, 56–61

'split-brain' patients 85

split-style drawings 25

standard deviation 172

Stanford prison simulation 99, 106–111

statistics 172–173

    alternative hypothesis 173

    bimodal data 172

    books 174

    causal link 173

    descriptive 172

    extreme scores 172

    inferential 172–173

    key concepts 174

    mean 172

    measures of central tendency 172

    measures of dispersion 172

    measures of variability 172

median 172

mode 172

multimodal data 172

null hypothesis 173

probability 172–173

range 172

significance level 173

significance table 173

skewed distribution 172

standard deviation 172

Type 1 error 173

Type 2 error 173

stereotyped pattern of behaviour 28

stereotypes 16

subject attrition 60

superego 63

suproxin 74

T

television violence 51, 55

thanatos 90

themes 8–9

theory of mind, autistic children 29, 30–31, 33

therapists 151

thinking like a psychologist

    (1) methods 6–7

    (2) themes 8–9

    (3) ethics 10–11

    books 12

    websites 12

two-factor theory 73

two-question condition 45, 47, 49

Type 1 [statistical] error 173

Type 2 [statistical] error 173

U

unethical research, most 105

universal language 15, 22–27

unsolicited participation 114

V

validity 9, 141, 145, 158, 162, 170

variability measures 172

visual illusions 22, 23, 25

W

Washoe (chimpanzee) 36–39

Wechsler-Bellevue Intelligence Scale 148

Wernicke's area 85

Weschsler Memory Scale 148

Wilcoxon test 164

withdrawal from investigation 11

'words' hemisphere of brain 84

World Health Organisation 141

'writing behaviour' 142–143

Z

Zimbardo prison study 99, 106–111